ELECTING JUSTICE

ELECTING JUSTICE

Fixing the Supreme Court Nomination Process

RICHARD DAVIS

OXFORD

UNIVERSITY PRESS

2005

OXFORD
UNIVERSITY PRESS

Oxford University Press, Inc., publishes works that further
Oxford University's objective of excellence
in research, scholarship, and education.

Oxford   New York
Auckland   Cape Town   Dar es Salaam   Hong Kong   Karachi
Kuala Lumpur   Madrid   Melbourne   Mexico City   Nairobi
New Delhi   Shanghai   Taipei   Toronto

With offices in
Argentina   Austria   Brazil   Chile   Czech Republic   France   Greece
Guatemala   Hungary   Italy   Japan   Poland   Portugal   Singapore
South Korea   Switzerland   Thailand   Turkey   Ukraine   Vietnam

Published by Oxford University Press, Inc.
198 Madison Avenue, New York, New York 10016

www.oup.com

Oxford is a registered trademark of Oxford University Press

Library of Congress Cataloging-in-Publication Data
Davis, Richard, 1955–
Electing justice : fixing the Supreme Court nomination process /
by Richard Davis.
    p. cm.
Includes bibliographical references.
ISBN-13 978-0-19-518109-8
ISBN 0-19-518109-3
1. United States. Supreme Court—Officials and employees—Selection
and appointment. 2. Judges—Selection and appointment—United States. I. Title.
KF8742.D383 2005
347.73'2634—dc22   2004015898

9 8 7 6 5 4 3 2

Printed in the United States of America
on acid-free paper

To my students, who have enriched my life
through the lessons they have taught me

Acknowledgments

The research conducted for this book could not have been completed without the assistance of many people involved in recent Supreme Court nominations who allowed me to interview them at length. I am particularly grateful to Justice Ruth Bader Ginsburg, Justice Stephen Breyer, and Judge Robert Bork, who graciously allowed me to interview them after they had experienced their own respective confirmation processes. Others who helped educate me on the nomination process (followed by their positions at the time of the interview) included Robert Katzmann, senior fellow at the Brookings Institution; Ralph Neas, executive director of the Leadership Conference on Civil Rights; Nan Aron, executive director of the Alliance for Justice; Tom Jipping, director of the Center for Law and Democracy at the Free Congress Foundation; Carl Cannon, White House correspondent for the *Baltimore Sun*; Joan Biskupic, U.S. Supreme Court correspondent for the *Washington Post*; Tony Mauro, U.S. Supreme Court correspondent for *USA Today*; Dennis Burke, legislative counsel to Arizona Senator Dennis DeConcini; and Utah Senator Orrin Hatch and his Judiciary Committee and personal staff. Still others wished to remain anonymous.

Brigham Young University colleagues Eric Schulzke, Matt Holland, John Fee, and David Magleby provided guidance, assistance, and support at various points in the research and writing stages. Former colleague Bud Scruggs was particularly helpful in enabling me to obtain interviews with key players. Kermit Hall and Lee Epstein reviewed the manuscript and offered critical insights. However, none of these individuals is responsible for any errors in this book. I alone am to blame.

Several research assistants helped over a number of years to further this research: Vincent James Strickler, Anna Nibley, Kristen Winmill Southwick, Xiao Xiaoying, Chad Fears, Angela Hermann, Erin Whitworth, Jennifer Hogge, Brady Long, Marc Turman, Erika Rahden, Dana Morrey, Rachel Williams, and Kristin Baughman. The College of Family, Home, and Social Sciences at Brigham Young University extended critical financial support for travel and research assistance.

Last, but hardly least, my family understood as I traveled frequently to Washington to examine documents, observe nomination process events, and interview key participants. Their unflagging support has been much appreciated.

Contents

ELECTING JUSTICE

Introduction

A Broken Process

On June 14, 1993, after introducing his first Supreme Court nominee to the nation in a Rose Garden ceremony, President Clinton turned the podium over to the 60-year-old Brooklyn-born judge. Ruth Bader Ginsburg gave a moving speech, including warm praise for her mother, and then closed with a touching self-challenge: "I pray that I may be all that she would have been had she lived in an age when women could aspire and achieve, and daughters are cherished as much as sons."

Tears welled up in the president's eyes as he and the audience gave Ginsburg warm, sustained applause. He was pleased. His announcement and Judge Ginsburg's short speech reinforced the White House's effort to show that the president had made history by choosing the second woman to the Court and a long-time legal activist for women's rights.

Then, according to the previously announced schedule, President Clinton turned to the press to take questions. The first, and ultimately only, question was asked by Brit Hume of ABC News. Hume, trying to be respectful, yelled toward the president from the edge of the Rose Garden:

The withdrawal of the Guinier nomination, sir, and your apparent focus on Judge Breyer and your turn, late, it seems, to Judge Ginsburg, may have created an impression, perhaps unfair, of a certain zigzag quality in the decision-making process here.

I wonder, sir, if you could kind of walk us through it and perhaps disabuse us of any notion we might have along those lines. Thank you.

Visibly annoyed by the question, Clinton responded curtly: "I have long since given up the thought that I could disabuse some of you of turning any substantive decision into anything but political process." The president warmed to his topic: "How you could ask a question like that after the statement she just made is beyond me." Then, probably anticipating further similar questions, President Clinton quickly began to escort Judge Ginsburg off the platform, signaling an abrupt end to the press conference.

Old Myths and New Realities

The exchange between the president and the journalist represents the ideal of the Supreme Court nomination process versus its present reality. The ideal is cherished in American culture. Many Americans would like to think the manner in which people become justices on the United States Supreme Court is governed by merit and objectivity.[1] They would like to think the president chooses the most qualified individual and the Senate confirms such a person promptly.

However, recent events suggest something very different. Supreme Court nominations have become public pitched battles involving partisans, ideological groups, single-issue groups, and the press. These groups and the media have taken center stage to argue less the merits of a nominee than political traits such as acceptability to particular issue groups, ideological bent, and appeal to the public. They declare that the nominee must be pro-choice or pro-life, sympathetic to the gay rights movement or hostile to its agenda, ideologically liberal or clearly conservative.

Individual nominees have been scrutinized for signs of agreement or disagreement with group agendas. Robert Bork was pilloried by liberal groups because of his views on privacy, abortion, and judicial review. Conservative groups challenged the potential nominations of Mario Cuomo and Bruce Babbitt in 1993 as liberal politicians who would undo the gains conservatives had made in the Rehnquist Court.

Not only has an actual vacancy activated these forces but also even the prospect of a Supreme Court nomination now resembles sharks smelling the scent of blood in the water. As groups face the reality of aging justices nearing retirement, a narrowly divided Senate, and an ideologically driven president, the battle is joined.

Early in George W. Bush's first term, the prospect for a major confirmation fight seemed imminent. With Republican control of both the White House and the Senate, the White House finally could press presidential nominees through the Senate Judiciary Committee and the Senate as a whole. The Republicans promised to expedite judicial nominees. Conservative interest groups pushed for the confirmation of favored judicial nominees. The Eagle Forum launched a major grassroots campaign to lobby the president to nominate and the Senate Judiciary Committee to confirm socially conservative judges.[2]

The Democrats lashed back, claiming partisanship. Senator Pat Leahy of Vermont charged: "Many see this as part of a partisan effort to pack the courts. This is not the way to discharge our constitutional duty to advise and consent."[3] Liberal groups urged Democrats to stop the movement of conservative justices onto the federal bench and sought to mobilize supporters to lobby their senators to oppose confirmation. NOW urged their grassroots supporters to "write or call your Senators and ask them NOT to confirm these nominees," while People for the American Way set up a Web site titled savethecourt.org.[4]

Democrats threatened to use their only viable remaining institutional weapon—the filibuster—knowing that if they held ranks a cloture vote would fail. Judiciary Committee chair Senator Orrin Hatch shot back: "If that starts, then that means that this will devolve into a total ideological exercise, which would be very unfortunate."[5] Nevertheless, Democrats filibustered appellate court nominees and promised to do so for an even bigger prize. Senate Minority Leader Tom Daschle warned Republicans that Democrats might use their tool even on a Supreme Court nominee:

> "I think it just depends on how qualified the nominee will be and if there is such an opening," he said. "If a replacement for the chief justice of the U.S. Supreme Court represents an extreme far-right position on most of the issues of the day, or issues relating to the Constitution, I think he or she would be in for a rough ride, in terms of the confirmation."[6]

Senators Daschle and Leahy urged the White House to open a "bipartisan process of consultation" when a Supreme Court vacancy appeared in order to help the president find a confirmable appointee. However, the White House press secretary quickly rejected the idea of discussing an appointment with senators and argued that "the Constitution is clear, and the Constitution will be followed."[7]

What these events indicate is that the mechanism of appointing Supreme Court justices looks little like the ideal the public envisions. Instead, it has become a public political battleground where groups wage holy war and the tactics reflect a no-prisoners approach to combat. One former senator compared the Senate's role in judicial selection to legislative lobbying, concluding that groups "have turned the confirmation process into something that's not very different than passing a bill."[8] Indeed, groups mobilize their members to pressure senators to vote for or against confirmation.

Like an Election

But a perhaps more accurate analogy is that of an electoral campaign. The similarities between presidential elections and judicial appointments are becoming increasingly apparent.

For example, presidential candidates are subject to intense press scrutiny over past and current public and private activities, including past drug use, sexual affairs, financial problems, and brushes with the law. So are Supreme Court nominees. Like a presidential candidate, the nominee's background is open to public scrutiny, including every past public statement, action, and affiliation. Even private activity is fair game. Video rental records and past girlfriends are not beyond the pale.

Candidate campaigns design elaborate image-making strategies for public consumption, complete with popular personal themes— "working class background," "leadership skills," or "executive experience." Similarly, the White House "sells" a nominee as representative of a certain group—women, Italian American, African American, Catholic—and/or pushes certain themes with nominees, such as the candidate is a "strict constructionist" who interprets the Constitution literally or the candidate reflects certain American values, such as the "pinpoint" strategy used by the George H. W. Bush administration to promote Clarence Thomas as a model of American success.[9]

Groups research presidential candidates' backgrounds to determine whether to endorse or oppose and then often devote extensive funding and other resources to reinforce their decisions. Similarly, groups tout or support Supreme Court nominees and are willing to spend large sums of their money to shape public opinion and win the eventual votes of senators.

The transformation of the Supreme Court appointment process into a mechanism similar to that of an electoral campaign has occurred because of the introduction of new, powerful players—the news media, interest groups, and public opinion. These forces now shape the system of judicial selection in a way unknown a half century ago.

This change into a quasi election is not unique. Other appointment processes in national politics also have undergone similar makeovers. Cabinet members now can face intense public scrutiny if significant opposition arises.[10]

However, the nature of the Court itself offers a qualitative difference. The small size of the institution, the longevity of the justices (life terms), and the policy-making power of the institution as a coequal branch makes such a transformation more dramatic than one involving a cabinet secretary who serves as an underling for the president and at the president's will.

It also moves further than other processes from the constitutional underpinnings that traditionally defined judicial selection. Although bureaucratic appointments ultimately are part of the executive branch and are accountable to the legislative branch—both governed by officials elected in partisan elections—the Court has been an institution apart in many ways, including personnel selection.

Constitutionally, the Court is the most distant institution from the public. So is the selection system of justices. The two bodies that constitute the formal selection process were designed to be one step removed from the public. Originally, the president was elected by the electoral college, the states' elites, and the Senate was elected by the state legislatures. Their role in judicial selection established a barrier between the Court and the public.

Today's process reflects the changes for the other players involved in judicial appointment. The president no longer enjoys the distance from the public envisioned by the framers. Rather, presidents are virtually directly elected by the voters in each state. Nor are senators as distant as they once were. They now are elected directly by the voters in their respective states. As the barriers between the public and the president and senators have fallen, the public has drawn one step closer to the judicial selection process.

Yet, today the public is not directly involved in the Supreme Court nomination process, which is a crucial difference between presidential elections and today's judicial selection process. All the trappings of mass electorate involvement exist, but in fact the electorate is still a body of essentially 101 people—the U.S. Senate, plus the president of the United States. That group is even smaller than the number of electors in the electoral college.

Of course, one could argue that in that sense presidential selection really is much like a Supreme Court nomination. The actual electors are not the 100 million people who vote in presidential elections, but the 535 individuals who constitute the electoral college—an elite much like the president and the Senate.

However, there are significant differences. The presidential electors are chosen by the state political party organizations and therefore nearly always personally support the victor of the popular vote in the state. Moreover, the moral expectations placed on electors are that they will vote for the candidate who wins the popular vote. (In some cases, the obligation hypothetically is stronger than an ethical one because 26 states legally *require* the electors to vote for the popular vote total winner.)[11] And historically, few electors actually have done otherwise, which suggests the compelling role of such an expectation.

Senators, on the other hand, have no such moral obligation to vote a certain way on a Supreme Court nominee. In fact, senators have voted for or against nominees when their constituencies seemingly did not approve. For example, Senator Alan Dixon of Illinois voted to confirm Clarence Thomas in 1991 and was defeated for reelection within six months by Carol Moseley Braun, who strongly opposed Thomas.

According to Alexander Hamilton in Federalist number 77, in fact, the elite nature of the body was its appeal when the framers sought a check on the president's power. No constitutional provision, state law, or Senate rule requires senators to represent their state populations in a vote on a Supreme Court nomination. Compared with electors, who are similar to automatons in the discharge of their constitutionally appointed duty, senators are inclined to play truly deliberative roles in their "advise and consent" function.

In a sense, selecting justices for the Supreme Court is an election without voters. Admittedly, the U.S. Constitution specifically excluded the voters, just as it did with presidential selection. Yet, over 200 years of history, and particularly in the last quarter century or so, we have transformed the judicial selection process into one with all of the trappings of an electoral campaign but without the key players—the electorate. This is an untenable situation—a reality that looks only vaguely familiar to the formal structure designed for it more than 200 years ago and a process that no longer reflects reality.

A Hybrid Process

The introduction of these new external forces—the media, groups, and the public—and the resulting quasi-election status of Supreme Court appointments have created a procedure divergent from that outlined in the Constitution. It produces a hybrid arrangement, where the constitutional requirements that favor elites and exclude the general public collide with the current version, in which external forces, including the general public, actually help determine the outcome. Although one solution might be to return to the elite-dominated process of yore, in fact, that is impossible. Rather, the formal outline of the process should conform to what the process actually has become.

External forces perform functions today that were not acknowledged originally in the Constitution. Selection of justices should be changed constitutionally to reflect the reality of external players rather than the false idea of exclusive elite involvement.

What is that reality? External players, not constitutionally enumerated, affect the conduct and outcome of the Supreme Court nomination process. My argument is not that these players were not significant before. In fact, these players have participated on infrequent occasions in the past. Examples include the nominations of Louis Brandeis in 1916 and John J. Parker in 1930, both of which stirred interest group involvement and public debate.[12]

But from the late 1960s on, their role has grown in intensity, particularly in selected nominations, and since the 1980s their involvement has become highly public. And it has extended to all Supreme Court nominations, not just occasional controversial ones. Not only are these forces players in the process but also their effect on the outcome of some nominations, such as those of Robert Bork and Clarence Thomas, is widely accepted.[13]

As a consequence, there is a significant difference between the process existing during most of U.S. history and the one in operation today. The difference is the extent and permanence of the role of these external players. As a result, Supreme Court nominations are highly public processes including new, and hardly shy, players. Their addition has altered the process of selecting Supreme Court nominees.

The legitimacy of these has grown gradually over the years but now has reached the point where their role goes unchallenged. The public vetting of candidates for presidential selection, White House and Senate consideration of interest group positions, and the extensive and highly public Senate investigation and hearing process all suggest that internal players have come to accept external forces as legitimate players in the process.

One response to this development is the argument that these players' involvement is merely an aberration. This argument suggests that at certain periods of American history, external players have entered the fray for brief periods. Examples are the failed nominations of candidates such as Abe Fortas (1968), Clement Haynsworth (1969), and G. Harrold Carswell (1970). Yet such instances are uncommon. Similarly, the argument goes, more recent controversial nominations such as those involving Clarence Thomas and Robert Bork were rare instances rather than part of a trend.

According to this theory, the public campaigns conducted by interest groups and the involvement of the media and public opinion in the nominations of Robert Bork, Douglas Ginsburg, and Clarence Thomas in the late 1980s and early 1990s could be viewed as isolated events. Indeed, the subsequent appearance of less controversial nominees such as Ruth Bader Ginsburg and Stephen Breyer would seem to be ample evidence that the elite-dominated process—that is, one controlled largely by Washington insiders, particularly the White House and the Senate—has reemerged. If this theory is correct, then we would expect that future nominees will escape the scrutiny accorded nominees in that period and that the judicial selection process will return to its elite-dominated state.

However, several signs point to continued high-profile conflict over the judicial selection process, which certainly spills over into Supreme Court nominations. One piece of evidence has been the recent treatment of nominations of lower federal judges. Lacking a Supreme Court nominee for a decade, both liberal and conservative groups sparred over federal appellate judicial nominees. During the George W. Bush administration, groups such as the Alliance for Justice, the AFL-CIO, and People for the American Way targeted nominees such as Charles Pickering, Patricia Owen, and Miguel Estrada.[14] Charles Pickering was labeled by these same groups as a racist and unworthy of the federal bench, although President Bush gave him a temporary recess appointment. Pro-choice groups labeled Owen "anti-abortion" because she upheld a parental notification law, although she was eventually confirmed.[15] Estrada was accused of being much more conservative than he would reveal in Senate Judiciary Committee hearings, resulting in a Senate filibuster and successive failed votes on his nomination.[16]

Similarly, conservative groups such as the Heritage Foundation and the Free Congress Foundation targeted Clinton nominees during his presidency and, while Republicans controlled the Senate, effectively blocked votes on many of them. Richard Paez, a nominee for the 9th Circuit Court of Appeals, waited four years before achieving Senate confirmation. Others saw their nominations die when Clinton's term in office ended.[17]

Another sign of the battle over the lower courts is the length of a nominee's wait for confirmation. Today, the average length of time between nomination of judicial candidates and confirmation is six months. In contrast, judicial nominees during Ronald Reagan's first term were confirmed on average in just one month.[18]

Rather than a sign that the battle has permanently shifted to lower courts, the lower court judicial selection struggles suggest that the battle over Supreme Court nominations will be just as vicious, if not more so, than those over lower court nominees. Interest groups promise similar fights over potential Supreme Court nominees. For example, conservative activist Phyllis Schlafly promised that conservative groups would oblige Republican presidents to nominate committed conservatives: "We are not going to put up with another [David] Souter."[19] The process is now, and will be for the foreseeable future, highly political and public. According to scholar William G.

Ross, "groups have become a permanent and prominent feature of the judicial selection process."[20]

Then what should be done? Reform of a process to acknowledge and adapt to its current form is difficult for our political system. However, changing our public official selection processes in order to reflect democratic trends is hardly a new feature of American politics. Both presidential and senatorial selection modes have been reformed to acknowledge democratic trends. These institutions have survived such change. Supreme Court justice selection similarly needs restructuring to reflect the permanent roles of these external players. That reform is essential, not just at the confirmation stage but also earlier, during the nominee selection process.

But before proposing specific solutions to this dilemma, it is necessary to back up and fully describe the problem at hand. What is the traditional process, and how has it been changed by the addition of these new players as permanent fixtures? What roles do these external players play today—both in the nomination stage and in the confirmation stage? Finally, what can be done to reform judicial selection to mesh constitutional structure with reality and preserve the trend of democratization?

1

Traditional versus New Players

The day President Woodrow Wilson announced the nomination of Louis Brandeis to a seat on the U.S. Supreme Court, the press cornered Brandeis at a social event and asked for his reaction. Brandeis replied: "I have not said anything and will not." Brandeis said a lot privately about the confirmation battle that swirled around him, but he steadfastly maintained his public silence.[1]

That was 1916. Today, no Supreme Court nominee would dare make such a statement. Instead, they would be required to sit before a phalanx of senators at a hearing broadcast live to the nation and answer questions for several days. They would be expected to answer lengthy questionnaires and, if necessary, appear with the president at press conferences.

It is difficult to remember that for most of our history the selection process for Supreme Court justices was characterized by its insularity. Until the latter part of the twentieth century, most nominations involved exclusively the White House, the Senate, and legal community leaders. Public controversy over nominees erupted on occasion, but typically the debate was joined by a relatively small number of insiders.

The process of confirming a justice today is a media-oriented exercise. White House management of a Supreme Court nomination reflects concern about the press portrayal of a nominee. Senators are well aware that television cameras in the hearing room are beaming their faces and words to millions of Americans, even tens of millions during controversial hearings, such as those held for Robert Bork and Clarence Thomas.

Group and press involvement—and their interaction as the press uses groups as news sources and groups use the press as a medium for communicating with others—draws the public into the process. Public opinion becomes the implicit gauge of selection and confirmation. A nominee who engenders the disapproval of the public would be a difficult call for the U.S. Senate. Obviously, such sentiment does not exist separate from the influence of elite messages in the form of White House image making, press coverage, and group response, but public opinion surveys and other less scientific measures such as letters to politicians, letters to the editor, and protests become tools for proponents and opponents in justifying appointment or rejection.

The public clearly become observers, particularly as the process is punctuated by media events such as presidential nomination, group reaction, and confirmation hearings. But the public serve as more than mere observers. The public's views—as expressed in public opinion surveys and interest group grassroots lobbying efforts—become factors in the decision making by the traditional players.

Traditional Players

The traditional process was dominated by the interaction of three players. The president nominated, the Senate confirmed (or not), and the justices of the Court both initiated the process (retirement or death) and were affected by it, since the process determined who sat with them on the Court.

Justice Ruth Bader Ginsburg once wrote: "Judicial confirmation is the extraordinary moment in which the three branches of government intersect."[2] The process of nominating Supreme Court justices indeed represents a nexus of the three branches of American national government. The Constitution provides for presidential appointment power over "judges of the Supreme Court" with the "Advice and Consent of the Senate."[3] No other constitutional responsibility so joins the three branches.

Historically, the traditional players had the process largely to themselves. There have been exceptions to this rule when various interest groups and press coverage influenced the outcome of presidential selection and/or Senate confirmation. Some of those instances are discussed here, but the permanent fixtures in the process have been the president, the Senate, and the Court itself.

Presidential Politics

For the president, Supreme Court appointments serve as significant historical marks of an administration. This is especially true of the appointment of chief justices, whose terms of service punctuate periods of the Court's history. But even appointments of associate justices can turn the tide of history. Two of the justices appointed by Franklin Roosevelt in the 1930s, William O. Douglas and Hugo Black, spearheaded the civil liberties orientation of the Warren Court. Lewis Powell served as a swing justice for many Court decisions during the 1970s and 1980s. The appointment of Clarence Thomas in 1991 at the age of 43 is likely to presage a lengthy career as a justice and the ability to influence Court decisions for decades into the future.

Because presidents have the potential of affecting policy for many years beyond their own limited terms, their tendency is to search for younger nominees who can serve for a significant amount of time. Richard Nixon suggested the ideal Supreme Court nominee is "between forty and fifty years of age. I think that ... sixty-year-old men would be a mistake."[4]

But in a more immediate sense, nominations to the Court determine the president's power to shape the judicial branch. Unlike lower level federal judiciary appointments typically driven by home state senatorial courtesy, the president participates directly in Supreme Court justice selection. Moreover, the appointment power allows the president to affect policy outcomes relative to the administration's immediate priorities. The Reagan and George H. W. Bush administrations, with appointments such as William Rehnquist as chief justice and Antonin Scalia, Anthony Kennedy, and Clarence Thomas as associate justices, were able to move the Court decidedly to the right, even during their presidential administrations.

These appointments also can reflect on the president's political standing vis-à-vis the legislative branch. On one hand, a successful, easy confirmation can reinforce the image of presidential success; on the other hand, failure to confirm presidential nominations suggests presidential incompetence in directing the Senate. Such battles have clear ramifications for the long-term relationship between a president and the Congress. It is probably not insignificant that one of the most unsuccessful recent presidents in obtaining confirmation of Supreme Court nominees (Richard Nixon) was also the only president to resign from office.

Even when presidents win confirmation for their nominees, a tough confirmation fight can deplete precious political capital. As an example, President George H. W. Bush won the struggle to confirm Clarence Thomas, but the effort ultimately contributed to the image of a weakened president. He faced a stiff primary challenge and ultimately lost his reelection bid.

In an era of plebiscitarian presidencies, public approval of the president, and therefore the president's power, often rises or falls based on singular high-profile events.[5] For example, both presidents Bush achieved soaring public approval ratings after Persian Gulf military victories.[6] And President Nixon faced a steady downward trend of public approval during the Watergate crisis, particularly after the release of tapes showing Nixon's role in the cover-up of the Watergate break-in. In the United States, popular approval ratings correspond to no-confidence votes in parliamentary governments. Although the president does not leave office as a prime minister does, the president may lose so much political capital that a mortal wound to the administration is inflicted.

One example is the case of President Bill Clinton, whose Supreme Court nominations were intended to help stanch the flow of bad press from administration mistakes, scandals, failed nominations, and unsuccessful legislative initiatives. For example, during the process to fill the Harry Blackmun vacancy in 1994, Clinton faced popular approval ratings hovering at 50 percent, and a major administration initiative, health care reform, faced stiff opposition. The White House hoped a popular Supreme Court nominee would reverse the perception of political failure, as well as the slide in the president's public approval rating.

Even the president's reelection effort may be affected by a Supreme Court nomination. Supreme Court appointments can be used to reach out to swing voters. In the fall of 1956, Dwight Eisenhower used a Supreme Court appointment to woo the votes of Democrats and Catholics by appointing New Jersey state judge William Brennan, a Catholic and a Democrat, to the Court.[7] While working in the Nixon White House, Pat Buchanan urged Richard Nixon only a year before Nixon's reelection to "appoint a conspicuous ethnic Catholic, like an Italian-American jurist with conservative views. Not blacks, not Jews, but ethnic Catholics, Poles, Irish, Italians, Slovaks."[8]

But an appointment also can be used to appease the president's core electoral constituency. George H. W. Bush's appointment of Clarence Thomas was designed to satisfy the right wing of the Republican Party as Bush launched his reelection campaign. The effort only partly succeeded, as Bush was wounded by the right-wing candidacy of Pat Buchanan in the Republican primaries and eventually lost his reelection bid.

The news portrayal of issues and events in national politics personalizes a Supreme Court nomination to the point that the president is inextricably bound to the success or failure of the nominee. Failure to confirm often produces the perception of presidential weakness, which in turn results in difficulties for the president in winning other contests with the Congress.

Thus, confirmation struggles have become major battlegrounds for presidents. Although historically four of five nominees have been confirmed (and the vast majority of those not confirmed were in the nineteenth century), since 1968, six of fifteen nominees have been rejected by the Senate or withdrew in the midst of controversy. Indeed, the period between 1968 and 1987 saw the defeat of three Supreme Court nominees by Senate vote (Clement Haynsworth, G. Harrold Carswell, and Robert Bork) and the withdrawal in the face of intense opposition of two others (Abe Fortas and Douglas Ginsburg). By contrast, only one nominee was defeated in the period 1901–1967 (John J. Parker).

Gaining confirmation has become a major objective of presidents in the wake of these rejections and the stakes involved. Hence, in recent years, presidents have devoted increased attention to management of nominations. Presidential management has become a more salient determinant than in the past in the confirmation success of a nominee.[9] The White House undertakes an aggressive task of selling the nominee to the Senate and to the nation. Because self-presentation of the nominee to the mass public has become far more critical than in the past, the White House has been intensively preparing nominees for not only Senate Judiciary Committee hearings but also all appearances before the press. Unlike in the nineteenth century and most of the twentieth, Supreme Court nominations are not quick processes that involve the president only at the decision-making stage.

Senate Role: "Advice and Consent" to Aggressiveness

The stakes are also high for the Senate. The Senate's role, long pendulum-like in its shift from sycophancy to aggressiveness, at this point in history leans more toward the latter (or at least the appearance thereof). The constitutionally prescribed "advice and consent" role now includes at least several weeks (or months) of staff investigation, committee hearings and final vote, and floor debate and final vote. Moreover, the pressures senators feel no longer emanate primarily from the legal community and only indirectly from the vast majority of constituents. Now the roles have reversed. Senators now face direct lobbying from constituents who have mobilized to affect the result.

Calls for Senate assertiveness in the nomination process began with Republican senators during the unsuccessful confirmation effort for Abe Fortas as chief justice in 1968. Senator Robert Griffin of Michigan reminded the Senate that the president's nomination was only part of the appointment process: "He's got only half the power. We've got the other half and it's time we asserted ourselves."[10] Calls became more frequent in the 1980s and 1990s, this time from Democrats who opposed Reagan and Bush nominees.[11] The press has summoned the Senate to sharply question nominees.[12] And, in response, the Senate has become more deliberative toward Supreme Court nominees in recent years, as measured by the length of time devoted to investigative research and the extent of questioning of the nominee. One scholar of confirmations concluded that the Fortas nomination significantly changed the Senate's attitude toward presidential nominees: "The presumption respecting presidential control was honored more in the breach than in the observance."[13]

One example is the contrast over time in the Senate Judiciary Committee's treatment of controversial Supreme Court nominees. In 1930, the Senate Judiciary Committee devoted one day of hearings to the controversial nomination of Judge John J. Parker as an associate justice. Parker himself never even testified.[14] However, nominees over the past 20 years have spent between three and five days on the witness stand, and other witnesses' testimony has taken from one to several days.

However, the danger is not all in one direction. The aggressiveness the Senate employs to scrutinize nominees can backfire. The Senate faces the danger of appearing belligerent. The mishandling of a Supreme Court nomination can damage the Senate's reputation, as demonstrated in the hearings involving Clarence Thomas and Anita Hill.

The Constitution is silent on what "advice and consent" means in the confirmation process. John Massaro's study of unsuccessful Court nominations concluded that ideology has been the main factor in Senate rejection.[15] But a vote centered explicitly on ideology may tarnish the process as too blatantly political. The Senate, then, walks a tightwire in judging Supreme Court nominees, with strong incentives to maintain balance throughout the process.

The Court's Role: Retirements, Court Functions, and Image Making

Obviously, the third major player with a stake is the Court itself. This may not seem obvious because, by outward appearances, the justices have little say in who joins their ranks, but the reality is much more complex. Like the other traditional players, the Court both affects and is affected by judicial selection.

The justices affect the process through timing. They typically control when they will leave the bench through retirement. Speculation often accompanies a justice's cryptic comments about retirement or the alignment of an aging justice, particularly one in poor health, with the incumbency of a president who reflects the justice's ideological views.

For instance, speculation was rampant immediately following the 2000 election because of the conjunction of several senior justices appointed by Republican presidents and a newly elected Republican president. Abetting this alignment was the strained atmosphere on the Court in the wake of the *Bush v. Gore* case settling the hotly disputed 2000 presidential election. The strident words contained in the variety of opinions issued by the Court in that case illuminated not only the importance of the Court in American political life but also the close divisions among the justices. Reportedly, the case of *Bush v. Gore* took an emotional toll on the justices and prompted Justice Sandra Day O'Connor to consider retirement.[16] Given O'Connor's prominent role as a swing justice over her tenure, the single vote of her replacement held the potential of being decisive in Court decision making for years to come.

Retirement of a chief justice attracts particular notice because Court eras tend to be marked by chief justices. And during this period another prospective retiree was Chief Justice William Rehnquist. Although the post carries only one of the nine votes on the court, the chief justice's power to assign opinions when in the majority and to determine a historical period offers the president an opportunity to shape the Court like no associate justice appointment.

The Court not only affects the appointment process but also is profoundly affected by it. Obviously, the appointment process determines who actually sits on the Court. Justices have no control over whom presidents select and senators confirm, yet that single individual (as one-ninth of the institution) can be a swing vote who shifts policy. Like most other people, sitting justices would like an additional colleague who thinks like them. Chief Justice Rehnquist once told a reporter: "You don't want eight of those people [who think like him] appointed, but, like all my colleagues, I would welcome two or three! If there were two or three people like me—I've been in dissent in a number of cases—perhaps some of those dissents would then become court opinions. That's a very iffy business, though."[17]

Moreover, that individual can affect the atmosphere on the Court. A tragic case was the appointment of James McReynolds, then U.S. attorney general, by President Woodrow Wilson in 1914. For the next 27 years, McReynolds's anticollegial behavior and outright anti-Semitism poisoned his relations with other justices and the general environment on the Court. McReynolds refused to acknowledge Jewish justices who spoke in conference and refused to participate in the annual Court photograph because it would require him to sit next to Justice Louis Brandeis, the first Jewish justice. Chief Justice Taft called him "a continual grouch," and when Chief Justice Harlan Stone remarked that an attorney's brief was the dullest one he had ever read, McReynolds replied: "The only thing duller I can think of is to hear you read one of your opinions."[18]

Yet there is even more than personnel selection in the effects on the Court. The Court's very prestige and power are affected by the conduct of the judicial nomination process. Reflecting the view of the institution, Henry Abraham argues that that process of judicial selection is one that must "assure [the justices] of independence, dignity, and security of tenure."[19]

But the current process has been criticized, particularly by the legal community, precisely for lack of dignity and the difficulty of maintaining the aura of independence throughout the proceedings.[20] One example is attention to the justices as individuals. Press and public attention to the nominees has extended far beyond the individual nominee's record or legal views to an examination of private activities. The stakes for the individual nominees are great as well—a seat on the Supreme Court or lasting infamy due to the characterizations attached to the nominee during the process.

Another dangerous area for the Court is the image of justices who are appointed to settle political scores or are the darlings of particular interest groups. For example, during the George W. Bush presidency, conservative groups urged the president to appoint Clarence Thomas as chief justice when Chief Justice Rehnquist retired, presumably to anger liberal groups for years to come.[21]

With its emphasis on the titillating and partisan, not surprisingly, confirmation coverage has not endeared the news media to the justices. Admittedly, news media coverage, particularly broadcast media, long has been problematic for the Court.[22] But, after tentative moves toward televised coverage of the Court, the justices rejected it. The cause, at least partly, was the nature of news coverage of the Robert Bork confirmation hearings.[23]

The Evolving Role of New Players

The Bork nomination is often viewed as a landmark because of the involvement of news media, groups, and public opinion. However, that nomination was not a first in that respect. External forces had participated in Supreme Court nominations previously. Both the press and groups were players in occasional confirmation battles.

Long before Robert Bork, press coverage had harmed a nominee's chances at confirmation. Alexander Wolcott, a customs tax collector, was nominated by President James Madison in 1811. Wolcott's appointment was panned by New England newspapers. One termed it "this abominable nomination." Another opined that Wolcott was said to be "more fit by far to be arraigned at the Bar than to sit as a judge." The newspaper condemnation undoubtedly was encouraged by Northern merchants who despised Wolcott because of his tax collector role. Wolcott was soundly defeated by the Senate.[24]

As Alexander Wolcott's story demonstrates, interest groups also intervened occasionally in the process, almost from the beginning of the selection process. That involvement arose on rare occasions throughout the nineteenth century. In 1881, railroad interests successfully lobbied President Rutherford B. Hayes to nominate Stanley Matthews, a former U.S. senator and a railroad's legal counsel. However, the nomination incurred the wrath of other economic groups. The New York Board of Trade and Transportation, a group representing 800 businesses, along with the National Grange and other farm groups, urged the Senate Judiciary Committee to defeat Matthews as too supportive of railroad interests.[25] Matthews eventually was confirmed. According to Henry J. Abraham, the fight over Matthews "marked the emergence of organized interest groups into the confirmation process of Supreme Court nominees."[26]

That involvement by the press and interest groups grew dramatically in the twentieth century, particularly in the wake of the Seventeenth Amendment providing for the direct election of U.S. senators. The first controversial nomination thereafter was President Woodrow Wilson's nomination of Boston lawyer and social advocate Louis Brandeis. Not only was Brandeis a distinguished Boston attorney who had acquired a reputation as an articulate social liberal but also he was Jewish and, if confirmed, would therefore become the first Jewish justice on the Court.[27]

Brandeis's nomination earned the ire of both conservatives and anti-Semites. Conservative forces mobilized to block confirmation by recruiting press support. The *New York Times*, the *Wall Street Journal*, and most New York newspapers editorialized against Brandeis's confirmation because he was viewed as a radical and therefore a threat to the social and political establishment.[28] However, other media outlets supported Brandeis. The *New Republic* editorialized in Brandeis's favor, and New York newspapers such as the *Independent* and the *New York World* were strong Brandeis supporters.[29]

Interest groups were prominent players in the Brandeis confirmation process. While business groups opposed Brandeis, labor groups weighed in to support the appointment. The legal community split, with many former bar association presidents opposing Brandeis, but law professors and law students lined up in his favor.[30] The Senate Judiciary Committee's lengthy public hearings called on witnesses both for and against confirmation. Interest groups sent letters to the committee to support a certain outcome from the committee and the Senate as a whole.[31]

In 1930, President Herbert Hoover's nominee John J. Parker stirred up even more controversy than Brandeis had. Although widely recognized as an outstanding jurist, Parker angered labor groups with an opinion perceived as antilabor. Parker claimed he was merely following Supreme Court precedent, but labor groups were not convinced.

Additionally, Parker angered the NAACP.[32] While running for governor a decade earlier, Parker had commented: "The participation of the Negro in politics is a source of evil and danger to both races."[33] When given the opportunity by the executive director of the NAACP to retract those views or at least clarify his current position, Parker declined, thus fanning the flames of opposition on civil rights grounds.[34]

An intense group lobbying effort deluged senators. Telegrams from labor groups and the NAACP urged senators to oppose the nomination. Black newspapers editorialized against Parker. The opposition of blacks was particularly disturbing for Republican senators because most African Americans at the time were allied with the Republican Party and the bloc vote of black voters was a significant electoral force in several Northern states.[35] The NAACP targeted several pro-Parker Republican senators for defeat in their next elections. A prominent black newspaper edited by W. E. B. Dubois listed all the senators who had voted for Parker and urged readers to work for their defeat.[36]

In turn, the White House attempted to recruit a group to endorse Parker. Long known for support of civil rights, the Society of Friends (Quakers) was pressured by Hoover, also a Quaker, to blunt the

NAACP's campaign. But the effort failed. Parker eventually was rejected by the Senate because he was perceived as having an antilabor and anti-Negro bias.[37] Parker went down to defeat.[38]

A few years later, newspaper editorials lambasted Franklin Roosevelt's appointment of Senator Hugo Black of Alabama. The *Chicago Tribune* opined that "if [Roosevelt] wanted the worst man he could find he has him."[39] The *Washington Post* charged that if Black "has ever shown himself exceptionally qualified in either the knowledge or the temperament essential for exercise of the highest judicial function, the occasion escapes recollection."[40] However, press opposition made little impact on the Senate, which confirmed Black handily. It was also the press that uncovered evidence of the extent to which Black had been associated with the Ku Klux Klan a decade earlier, but only after Black had already been confirmed.[41]

Nor did interest groups gain much sway in nominations after their success in defeating Judge Parker. For example, several women's groups including the Young Women's Christian Association (YWCA), the American Association of University Women (AAUW), and the Business and Professional Women (BPW) lobbied Franklin Roosevelt to nominate Florence Allen to the Court in the late 1930s, but Roosevelt saw little political gain in satisfying these groups.[42]

External force involvement did not reemerge until the 1960s. By this point, group testimony was a given during Senate Judiciary Committee hearings. For example, during the confirmation hearings for Abe Fortas as chief justice in 1968, the Senate Judiciary Committee invited leaders of four interest groups to testify, including one from Citizens for Decent Literature who testified that Fortas had ruled in favor of obscenity in 49 cases. Twelve groups testified during committee hearings for Clement Haynsworth the next year.[43]

The change toward a greater role for the press, interest groups, and public opinion has been gradual—with certain nominations such as those of Louis Brandeis and John J. Parker as seminal events. But there is a critical difference between the past quarter century of Supreme Court nominations and the previous nearly 200 years: External force involvement clearly has increased to the point of a significant and permanent role today rather than an occasional appearance. Earlier periods and today offer stark contrasts in the role of groups, the news media, and public opinion.

Groups

Interest group role today, as opposed to earlier in the twentieth century, is considered legitimate. Witnesses in the Brandeis hearing did not include interest groups. It was not until the Parker nomination in 1930 that groups were invited to testify at confirmation hearings."[44] Today, group representatives are a staple of committee hearings, even in less controversial nominations. Interest groups such as the Alliance for Justice, the National Abortion Rights Action League (NARAL), and the National Organization for Women (NOW) on the left and the Institute for Justice, the Family Research Council, and Concerned Women for America on the right are expected witnesses in the Senate's information-gathering process.

In the past, individual senators would have heard on occasion from group representatives, particularly those from their states. Of course, that became difficult in the numerous cases when confirmation occurred within days, sometimes even within hours, of a presidential nomination. Today, senators expect groups to weigh in on nominees via mail, fax, telephone calls, and e-mail, not to mention personal lobbying. In the past, interest groups sent letters to senators urging a vote for or against a nominee. But today groups use an arsenal of weapons to shape Supreme Court nominations, including advocacy ads, op-ed columns, interviews with group leaders, and press releases.

The News Media

In earlier nominations, the press at times editorialized on confirmation. But press coverage of nominees was limited by the lack of resources for covering a Supreme Court nomination. Editorials became the medium for supporting or opposing a nominee.

Now the news media uncover Supreme Court nominees as they do presidential candidates or cabinet appointments. Intense press scrutiny accompanies the announcement of a nominee. In fact, such scrutiny occurs even before a presidential selection, when names of potential nominees are floated by the White House or various groups.

Moreover, interest groups in the past used the press only occasionally to reach the public. A more effective means was the direct route to senators. Today, the effort to draw in the press and the public is expected, particularly after the high-profile success of opposition groups in the Bork nomination and the high-profile effort of interest groups on both sides in the Thomas nomination.

Public Opinion

Until the last quarter century or so, the public's role was minimal in Supreme Court confirmations. Some groups engaged their supporters to defeat the Parker nomination, yet such involvement was rare. In many cases, the brief period between presidential nomination and Senate confirmation meant the public did not even know a nomination had occurred until after (or at the same time) confirmation took place.

The direct election of senators opened the door to public involvement. However, the extent of such involvement was limited for some time. Even in the case of the Brandeis confirmation, the main players were the legal community and groups rather than the public generally. The Parker nomination more than a decade later was the first instance of public involvement, albeit still limited compared with today's confirmation processes.

One barrier to using public opinion in affecting confirmation outcomes was the absence of measures to assess broad public sentiment. The scientific measurement of public opinion did not gain widespread use until the 1930s.

Another barrier was lack of a vehicle for public information. Until 1930, the Senate Judiciary Committee held secret sessions on Supreme Court appointments (with only a few exceptions such as the Brandeis

nomination). Although other Senate hearings were aired on television beginning with the 1950s, hearings on Supreme Court nominees
were not televised until 1981.

But the greatest change has been in widespread elite acceptance
of the legitimacy of public responsibility in assessing Supreme Court
nominees. Such a role was questionable even as late as the Parker
nomination in 1930. When Parker was defeated by the Senate, President Herbert Hoover drafted a public statement claiming that the confirmation "was opposed by a vigorous nation-wide propaganda from
different groups among our citizens" who have "carried the question
of confirmation into the field of political issues rather than personal
fitness." Hoover concluded that "public opinion as a whole cannot
function in this manner."[45]

Only several decades later was such involvement no longer
publicly challenged. Today, no president or senator would claim as
Hoover did that public opinion should not matter. In his landmark
study of interest group role, John Maltese concluded that since the
1980s, elite players in the process "pay much more attention to the
mobilization of public opinion than participants ever did in the nineteenth century."[46]

Today's Nomination Process

The process of nominating Supreme Court justices in recent years
might look unrecognizable to participants in the process 100 or even
50 years ago. In the past, presidents typically received recommendations from their staff, the legal community, and even sitting justices
and then issued a statement to the Senate nominating someone to the
Court. The Senate usually held low-key hearings or even bypassed
them to offer swift confirmation. Even when opposition occurred,
it was usually elements of the legal community acting privately to
oppose the nomination.

In contrast, over the past quarter century, live television coverage
of Senate hearings, "murder boards" in preparation for those hear-

ings, a flood of press releases, television and radio advertisements, and public opinion polls all characterize nominations. In addition, the president makes the announcement the subject of a major appearance before the press, with the nominee typically standing at the podium, and the president actively lobbies the Senate, the press, and the public to support the nominee.

These traits of public appearances, use of the press, and dependence on measures of public opinion are not new to the selection process for other offices in American politics. They have characterized the nomination and election processes of public officials, especially presidents. News media coverage, particularly with the emphasis on personal character, has dominated presidential electoral campaigns. As a result, issues such as adultery, military service, and prior drug use have emerged as major themes of recent presidential candidacies, as covered by the press. Presidential candidates now endure microscopic investigation of some aspects of their private lives, as do cabinet nominees and sometimes even candidates for other offices, such as governor or the U.S. Congress. For nominees to the U.S. Supreme Court, all of this is much more recent and still somewhat foreign. Like the sitting justices, nominees in the past were usually accorded a measure of public respect and media avoidance. But this is no longer true.

Like presidential candidates, Supreme Court nominees today are subject to exhaustive examination of their public records—papers, speeches, articles, decisions. But public scrutiny has gone beyond matters of public record. Their private lives, including past marriages and divorces (or the lack of marital status), financial records, and even video-watching habits have been examined. Senator Joseph Biden, Senate Judiciary Committee chair through two of the most contentious confirmations in U.S. history, reviewed examples of the effects of this disturbing trend: "Judge Bork had his video rental records exhumed and studied for possible rental of pornographic films. Judge Souter has his marital status questioned and felt obligated to produce ex-girlfriends to testify to his virility. Judge Thomas was assaulted by a whispering campaign that spread unsubstantiated rumors about the cause of the end of his first marriage."[47] Other nominees' personal backgrounds were almost remarkable precisely because they seemed to include no odd quirks (Anthony Kennedy, 1988; Ruth Bader Ginsburg, 1993; and Stephen Breyer, 1994).

Some individuals such as Robert Bork and Douglas Ginsburg have failed at confirmation because of this scrutiny. Others, however, win the confirmation, but also suffer opprobrium, at least for a time. After taking his seat, Clarence Thomas's opinions were scrutinized to reveal his views on sexual harassment in the wake of Anita Hill's charges during his confirmation hearings. Stephen Breyer's conflict of interest over a Lloyd's of London investment and his role in the construction of a new federal judiciary building in Boston, first raised during his confirmation hearings, continued to be an issue during his first year on the Court.[48]

The prospect of public exposure endured by recent nominees may have become a significant factor in the withdrawal of likely candidates for vacancies.[49] It has become almost conventional wisdom that nominees possess some character flaw that will emerge in the process and seriously jeopardize, if not fatally damage, their chances of earning confirmation. The nominee's opponents search for it while supporters steel themselves against its appearance. But private character is not alone as an object of group, press, and public scrutiny. The ideology of the nominee has acquired a greater public role in the nomination process. Interest groups scour the nominee's record to determine whether the justice-to-be heeds or strays from their own agendas. As well, some senators openly admit the significance of a nominee's ideological leanings in their eventual vote.

One by-product of this examination procedure has been the nomination of stealth candidates—nominees who have a short public record, particularly on issues of concern to interest groups. During the Reagan and first Bush administrations, successful nominees were those lacking any previous public position on abortion. Similarly, during the Clinton administration, scrutiny focused on the nominee's ties to extreme liberal groups and stances. However, the two Clinton Supreme Court nominees had somewhat mixed public records in terms of ideological direction on high-profile current public issues.

The nomination process has become an exhaustive journey for nominees. It means running through a maze of press and interest group scrutiny and public disclosure. It is almost a wonder anyone chooses to endure it. One legal scholar predicted that the legacy of the Robert Bork nomination would be to "treat a confirmation as if it were an election campaign, a media event complete with an avalanche of stump speeches and a bombardment of negative advertising, all accompanied by extensive direct mail advertising, campaign buttons, and solicitation of funds."[50]

As this process has emerged in recent years, criticism naturally has accompanied it. Deriding the direction of some of the confirmation processes of Supreme Court nominees during his Senate career, Senator Biden argued that "the nation is enriched when we explore their jurisprudential views; it is debased when we plow through their private lives for dirt."[51]

Not surprisingly, these developments have produced an intense debate over the role of the confirmation process itself. Critics charge that the confirmation process fails to serve its intended purpose. Rather than achieve the result of placing on the nation's highest court the most qualified individuals, the process has become a political donnybrook. To a great extent, the nomination process always has been a political exercise because political players dominate the process. But the business of appointing justices more recently has become blatantly so. On the heels of the Bork nomination, David P. Bryden wrote: "The battle over Bork was fought and won on political grounds. No one with even a modicum of political experience supposes that jurisprudential arguments were as influential as calls from constituents."[52]

The general public and the elites involved in the process expect at least the image of the process to be one of propriety and sobriety rather than naked power grabs by factions. Some of the recent nomination struggles have appeared more like the latter than the former.

Who's to Blame and What Is the Solution?

Much of the blame for the degeneration of the process has been placed on the Senate's investigation of nominees. The Senate's role is targeted precisely because it is the most public stage of the Supreme Court appointment process. But the criticism of the Senate's role is bifurcated.

Some critics, especially conservatives, have charged the senators on the Judiciary Committee with asking inappropriate questions of nominees—questions designed to elicit indications of future votes and even promises to vote in certain ways favored by the senator.[53] Another criticism, again generally made by conservatives, accuses senators of seeking specific legal outcomes rather than examining legal reasoning. President George H. W. Bush asserted that the Senate hearings in the Thomas nomination "bore little resemblance to the tidy legislative process that we all studied in school. . . . And the process seemed unreal—more like a satire . . . ; more like a burlesque show than a civics class."[54]

These critics favor a more limited role for the Senate—as a check only on those singularly unqualified to sit on the bench. Conservative commentator Bruce Fein argues the purpose of the confirmation process "is not to educate the Senate and the public at large: it is to screen out unfit characters."[55]

However, other critics have suggested the Senate has hardly done enough.[56] According to this camp, the Senate has failed to aggressively question nominees who slipped through without fully revealing their tendencies, and not enough emphasis is placed on the nominee's moral philosophy.[57] One news reporter argued that the Bork nomination was the kind of public process that should be followed in all confirmations.[58]

Liberals direct their attack on presidents Reagan and George H. W. Bush, who, they charge, politicized the process by proposing highly ideological nominees. They argue that when presidents require litmus tests of nominees—such as holding a certain position on abortion—the process has been corrupted well before the Senate receives the nomination. Conservatives respond that the blame rests squarely with leftist groups, including abortion rights and women's groups, who have adopted a strictly ideological approach to Supreme Court nominees.

With criticism often comes a plethora of suggested reforms. Many have emerged since Robert Bork's failed confirmation process. One scholar suggested allowing the president to initiate constitutional amendments in order to give the president more power to change constitutional law without having to resort primarily to judicial appointments.[59] Another suggested president-based reform is a requirement of consultation with the Senate prior to a nomination.[60] Some proposals deal with the Senate's role in the process in a formal way, such as requiring a two-thirds majority for confirmation, whereas others focus on the behavior of senators, such as no longer questioning nominees on their views on issues or not even questioning them at all.[61] Other recommendations involve the Senate's relationship with external groups, such as the banning of televised coverage of Senate Judiciary Committee hearings. Still others propose changes by both the president and the Senate.[62] But these solutions have also been critiqued as inadequate and perhaps even likely to do more damage.[63]

Public or Private?

These proposed reforms fall short because they ignore the origins of the dilemma—that is, the expanded roles of external players in the process. The direction of much of the proposed reform of the nomination process is toward reprivatizing the process by placing it once again in the hands of elites and outside the realm of the public. In some ways, it is a desire to depoliticize the process by draining it of its political component. But such an effort, according to William G. Ross, is likely "to promote hypocrisy and erode accountability."[64]

Depoliticizing and reprivatizing are simply not possible. The genie cannot be put back into the bottle. Once made public, the nomination process cannot then be transformed back to an elite-dominated procedure, any more than the public will stand for state legislative selection of U.S. senators or elimination of a linkage between the selection of state electors and the popular vote for president.

A more pragmatic approach is first to understand the part played by these external players and then to address the excesses emanating from such roles. Second, one must devise a process that recognizes, legitimizes, and regulates the position of external players, particularly the electorate.

The process of nominating a Supreme Court justice irrevocably has become public rather than private. And there it will stay. Any reform must acknowledge that fact rather than attempt to disregard it. Understanding the role of external forces and then adapting to it should be the goal of reform. That is the only practical solution.

But before we can explain how external forces affect Supreme Court nominations, we must understand why they care to do so. In other words, how and why are Supreme Court appointments so political?

2

The Politics of Judicial Selection

On July 1, 1795, President George Washington wrote a fateful letter to John Rutledge, a former associate justice of the U.S. Supreme Court. Chief Justice John Jay had just resigned after being elected governor of New York, and Washington was writing to tell Rutledge he was nominating him to be Jay's successor. Rutledge had wanted the appointment since Jay had been appointed six years earlier. In fact, once he heard of Jay's election, Rutledge had written to the president offering his services.

But in between the time Washington wrote his letter and Rutledge received it, word of the provisions of the Jay Treaty, a controversial compact with Great Britain, circulated around the nation and raised the ire of citizens of Charleston, South Carolina. During that period, Rutledge became a vocal opponent of the Jay Treaty by participating in a public meeting to oppose the treaty and subscribing to a strongly worded statement condemning the agreement between the United States and Great Britain. Washington and the Federalists who controlled the U.S. Senate strongly supported the Jay Treaty. Once Rutledge's position on the Jay Treaty became widely known, Federalists responded angrily. Opposition to Rutledge's confirmation grew. Thomas Jefferson wrote: "The rejection of Rutledge by the Senate is a bold thing, for they cannot pretend any objection to him but his disapprobation of the Treaty."

Not only was Rutledge attacked by the Federalist press for his opposition to the Jay Treaty but also newspaper articles questioned

his mental competence and emotional stability. Newspapers insinu-
ated erratic behavior on Rutledge's part. Even though Republican
newspapers defended him, charging that Washington knew Rutledge
well when he nominated him, the Federalist-controlled senate failed
to confirm.[1] Rutledge became the first federal judicial appointment to
be rejected by the Senate.[2]

Rutledge's politically motivated confirmation process was only
the first of many judicial selection battles animated by politics. A
number of subsequent presidents have seen their Supreme Court
nominees defeated for political reasons. All but one of John Tyler's
nominees failed to achieve Senate confirmation—all rejected for
political reasons.[3]

In accordance with the political nature of those players involved
in the process—the president and senators—politics has driven many
presidential selections and Senate reactions.

One political factor in presidential selections is the prospective
nominee's views on policy areas considered important to the president. Franklin Roosevelt wanted justices who would support the New
Deal. Richard Nixon favored social conservatives who would undo
or at least weaken some of the rulings of the Warren Court in areas
such as rights of the accused, school prayer, and school desegregation.
Nixon even specified that his nominee "must be against busing, and
against forced housing integration."[4] During the Reagan administration and both Bush administrations, a pro-life position on abortion
was a key criterion. Similarly, for Bill Clinton a pro-choice position
on abortion was a must.

Similarly, the Senate confirmation process has centered on a nominee's political views. For example, G. Harrold Carswell, nominated
by Nixon, was publicly labeled a racist when a 20-year-old speech
turned up in which Carswell proclaimed that he held a "firm, vigorous belief in the principles of White Supremacy, and I shall always
be so governed."[5]

Policy positions have not been the only factor. The political background of the individual shapes the process of both selection and confirmation. For example, President Clinton wanted an appointee who

had been a politician. However, such a political appointee raised red flags for opponents. New York Governor Mario Cuomo, Secretary of the Interior Bruce Babbitt, and Senator George Mitchell of Maine, all considered by President Clinton, clearly would have brought with them a political record pointing to a partisan bias. Such a record would be fodder for opponents in a confirmation process. Moreover, a politician might be more suspect of injecting politics into Supreme Court decision making and therefore using decisions to reach political objectives.

Ironically, as the Supreme Court appointment process has increasingly been viewed as publicly political, the odds of a politician even being nominated have diminished. The percentage of Supreme Court justices with previous careers primarily in politics has steadily declined, from a majority in the late 1800s to only 27 percent 100 years later.[6] The last former member of Congress to serve on the Supreme Court, Hugo Black, retired in 1971. Since Black, only one justice has ever served in elective office (Sandra Day O'Connor served six years in the Arizona State Senate). None of the others has served more than a small fraction of their careers in political appointments. The Court is not populated today by politicians but almost exclusively by former lower level judges.

The Court's own attempt to distance itself from politics while becoming integral to policy making has encouraged an attitude of public separation. This monkish existence is hardly attractive to most politicians. Mario Cuomo declined to be considered by the Clinton administration. Twenty years earlier, Senator Howard Baker similarly expressed reluctance about joining the Court.[7]

Another factor has been timing. Unsuccessful nominees often are those with the unfortunate circumstance of being nominated in the last throes of a dying administration. John Quincy Adams, James Buchanan, Rutherford Hayes, and Lyndon Johnson saw their nominees go down in defeat in the final months or even weeks of their terms.

Sour relations between Congress and the president have doomed some nominees. President Andrew Johnson nominated a well-respected candidate in former U.S. Attorney General Henry Stanbery.

Not only was Stanbery not confirmed but Congress eliminated the vacancy on the Court by reducing the number of justices from ten to nine. Congress soon impeached Johnson, who had angered the radical Republicans in Congress with his pro-Southern sympathies.[8]

Also, some nominations have fallen because of spite over past behavior of the principals in the nomination process. Following the filibuster of the vote on Fortas as chief justice in 1968, Democrats were upset over Republican tactics. When Richard Nixon nominated Clement Haynsworth in 1969 and ethical violations surfaced, Democrats seized their opportunity to elicit revenge.[9] Nixon responded in kind with the selection of a nominee—G. Harrold Carswell—that one scholar termed "an act of vengeance."[10] The Senate defeated that nominee as well. Similarly, conservative groups wanted revenge following the defeat of Robert Bork and their perception of unfair treatment of Clarence Thomas in 1991.

Because the confirmation phase is more public than the presidential selection stage, the former is more commonly labeled a political process. A *Washington Post* reporter, referring to the presidential nomination stage in 1994, termed the process "pre-politicized" in the sense that the political process over the nominee occurred prior to the president's announcement and not during the confirmation stage.[11]

Actually, politics is critical in both parts of the Supreme Court appointment process: presidential selection and Senate confirmation.[12] The second stage has been addressed in the literature far more than the first, but the first is no less political.[13]

Presidential Selection

Presidential selection of a nominee ideally involves the president surveying the legal community and choosing among the most capable members those who possess the merits to hold appointment to the Supreme Court. The mythology portrays the president as searching for a philosopher-king look-alike—wise, judicious, experienced, and above political pressures.

The rhetoric accompanying presidential appointments suggests this process dominates presidential decision making. When announcing the nomination of Sandra Day O'Connor on July 7, 1981, President Reagan called her a "person for all seasons, possessing those unique qualities of temperament, fairness, intellectual capacity, and devotion to the public good which have characterized the 101 brethren who have preceded her."[14] President George H. W. Bush went further and declared that his selection process resulting in the nomination of Clarence Thomas produced "the best person for this position."[15] Even George Washington was not immune to rhetorical excess. He remarked that one of his aforementioned nominees, John Rutledge, who had served as a delegate to the Constitutional Convention, actually "wrote the Constitution."[16]

However, the reality is something different. Presidents use a variety of selection criteria, with merit usually necessary but hardly sufficient. Historically, the most important criterion has been the fit between the ideology of the president and that of the nominee.

Selection Criteria

Ideology

In mulling their nominee choices, most presidents have been driven by the way history will treat them in terms of their impact on policy. Because they can nominate Supreme Court justices, as well as the rest of the federal judiciary, they know their impact extends beyond the executive branch to the judiciary as well. Most presidents have viewed appointments to the Supreme Court as an opportunity to place their distinctive stamp on the shaping of the law. President Reagan articulated this approach to appointments: "Those who sit in the Supreme Court interpret the laws of our land and truly do leave their footprints on the sands of time. Long after the policies of Presidents and Senators and Congressmen of any given era may have passed from public memory, they'll be remembered.[17]

Such efforts to mold the Court, and therefore policy, date from George Washington, who favored Federalists in his judicial appointments.[18] That approach to justice picking has hardly abated with recent presidents, who have continued to seek the appointment of justices sharing their partisanship and ideology. Richard Nixon articulated this tendency to judge a nominee's ideology in a speech: "I am more interested in the judicial philosophy than I am in what part of the country they come from and whether they are a woman or whether they are a man."[19]

Henry J. Abraham argues that the political and ideological compatibility of the nominee with the president has been "the controlling factor" in the selection process.[20] One measure of ideological correlation is partisanship. Presidents rarely choose nominees of the opposing party. Since 1961, only one of 13 justices appointed to the Court has not shared the partisan affiliation of their nominator.[21]

Ideology may be a factor in the tendency of recent presidents to appoint federal appellate judges to the bench. According to David Yalof, this trend of appointing federal judges to the Supreme Court may be related to the accuracy of the gauge of a federal judgeship in predicting how a nominee will rule once on the Supreme Court. Federal court judges handle many of the types of issues they would address as Supreme Court justices.[22]

The expectation of presidents that their nominees, once seated on the bench, will share their perspectives is evidenced by the reaction of some presidents to those nominees who have disappointed them. President Harry Truman was upset when the Court ruled against him in a case involving federal government control of the steel industry. Justice Byron White turned conservative once on the Court and disappointed the more liberal President John Kennedy, who had appointed him, and Attorney General Robert Kennedy, who had recommended him. The most egregious example was the vote by three of Richard Nixon's appointees against his position in the 1974 *U.S. v. Nixon* case. The decision to force Nixon to turn over the Watergate tapes led to his resignation.[23] Expectations of conformity to the president's views led Harry Truman to conclude that "when ever you put a man on the Supreme Court he ceases to be your friend. I'm sure of that."[24]

Despite their importance, political and ideological compatibility are not alone as significant criteria in the selection process. According to Henry Abraham, there are at least three others—objective merit, personal friendship, and representativeness—all of which have played critical roles in Supreme Court nominations.[25]

Merit

The first on the list, objective merit, is not unimportant for presidential consideration. The candidate for the Court must be widely viewed as meritorious (and not just by the president), or confirmation is unlikely. When a nominee is found wanting in this category—as was Judge Carswell (1970)—the nomination is unsuccessful.

However, there is little consensus on what constitutes objective merit. The range of personal backgrounds the justices who have served on the Court have brought with them challenges the notion that any single type of experience—judicial, legal, political, or administrative—guarantees either success or failure on the bench.

Even previous judicial experience has not necessarily been a gauge of effective judicial role. For example, Eisenhower appointee Charles Whittaker seemed ideal for the Court. He had served as both a federal district judge and a federal appellate court judge before his elevation to the highest court in 1957. But Whittaker was a major disappointment as a justice. He resigned in broken health after only five years on the Court. One of his colleagues explained that Whittaker couldn't handle the life of a justice because he "changed his mind so often."[26]

Conversely, another Eisenhower appointee, Chief Justice Earl Warren, is widely viewed by scholars as one of the greatest justices on the Court. Yet, the former California governor and Republican vice presidential candidate had never served as a judge prior to his appointment. Neither had John Marshall, Joseph Story, Roger Taney,

Louis Brandeis, Harlan Stone, and Felix Frankfurter—all of whom have also been considered great justices.[27]

The definition of merit has been vague, but one form of standardization has been introduced through the endorsement of the American Bar Association (ABA). As an independent body, the ABA offers an evaluation of nominees during the confirmation process. The ABA grading includes three categories—well qualified, qualified, and not qualified. Because other players pay attention to the ABA's rating of a nominee, the organization assumes a quasi-official role in the confirmation process.[28]

Presidents need not consider the ABA's evaluation, although they did so routinely for the last half of the twentieth century, even allowing the organization an opportunity to confidentially evaluate possible federal judicial nominees before they were publicly announced. This process gave the president an opportunity to gauge the organization's reaction to a potential nominee.

However, when the ABA leaked names of President Nixon's list of possible nominees, presidents began to distrust the ABA, and the practice of prior notice of Supreme Court appointments ended.[29] Shortly after taking office in 2001, the Bush administration eliminated the organization's role in the selection process of lower federal judges as well, arguing that continuing the ABA's "preferential, quasi-official role in the nomination process would be unfair to the other groups that also have strong interests in judicial selection."[30] The move was widely viewed as the culmination of conservative groups' long-standing complaints that the ABA was biased against conservative judicial nominees in its rating role.[31]

The ABA still plays a role in the process, just not at the presidential selection stage. Individual senators still use the ABA as a measure of merit because it offers an independent review of nominees designed to recognize merit (or its absence) in the appointment process and, ostensibly, is separate from the politics of presidential selection and Senate consideration. Therefore, the ABA's designation still can be a significant source of support for either supporters or opponents.

Either way, it also serves as a legitimation of the role of merit in the selection process.

Journalists note and editorialists opine on the designation awarded the candidate. Failure to earn the highest designation may lead to questions about the fitness of the nominee. However, the ABA's failure to award the highest status to a nominee does not necessarily doom confirmation chances. For example, Clarence Thomas was confirmed despite the ABA's designation as only "qualified," not "well qualified" (the highest designation).

The significance of the designation is shown by its ability to screen nominees. The ABA gave an "unqualified" designation to two of Richard Nixon's potential nominees. Although Nixon had not concluded at that time whether he would appoint them, he ultimately did not.[32] No successful nominee has failed to receive the organization's "qualified" designation. The highest designation, with its imprimatur for the legal community, is a coveted status for nominees.

Despite the ABA's statements that evaluations are limited to the criterion of "integrity, competence, and judicial temperament," the ABA's image as a neutral evaluator has been tarnished in the past.[33] The most visible example was the evaluation of Judge Robert Bork in 1987. While most of the ABA evaluating committee graded Bork as "highly qualified," four members rated him "unqualified." The dissenters' rationale was based primarily on ideological grounds and undermined the image of the association as heedless of such considerations.[34]

Friendship

Friendship with the nominee has been an important criterion for some presidents. Two recent presidents—Harry Truman and Lyndon Johnson—preferred their own friends for vacancies. All of Truman's appointees to the Court were personal friends.[35] Johnson appointed his good friend Abe Fortas as an associate justice in 1965 and then nominated him to be chief justice three years later during Johnson's last year in office. To replace Fortas as associate justice, Johnson selected another old friend from Texas, Homer Thornberry.

Johnson's effort to place his cronies on the Court backfired. Republicans led intense criticism of the nominees, based on ideological grounds but on friendship with the outgoing president as well. Republicans hoped they could delay a vote on the nominees and allow a new Republican president to select the new chief justice. Senate Republicans successfully blocked Fortas's confirmation, leading the associate justice eventually to withdraw his name from consideration.

As a consequence, succeeding presidents have been wary of attempts to nominate friends to the Court. For recent presidents, friendship with a Supreme Court nominee has become a less important factor. President Clinton once considered appointing a personal friend, Judge Richard Arnold of Arkansas, to the Supreme Court. However, the selection process occurred in the wake of extensive criticism of cronyism within the Clinton administration. Clinton had been accused of placing his or his wife's friends in high places in the administration. Arnold's chances would have been diminished precisely because of his proximity to Clinton, and Arnold was bypassed.

Representativeness

According to Article III, Supreme Court justices are responsible for deciding "all cases, in law and equity, arising under this Constitution." Because their mandate seems limited to deciding the cases before them and they are appointed for life, never face election or reelection, and never appear on any party ticket, representation of interests in society would not seem important.

However, representativeness long has shaped Supreme Court nominations. An early form of representativeness was regional balance on the Court. In the early years of the Supreme Court, the justices were appointed according to region of origin. Three of President George Washington's appointments to the original six-member court were from the South, and the other three hailed from northern states.[36] When a Massachusetts native retired from the Court, President James

Madison insisted that the replacement be a New Englander.[37] Southern-ers were sensitive about representation on the Court, particularly as tensions increased over slavery, and insisted on equal representation.

Regional balance was no small matter prior to the Civil War, and it ultimately shaped Court decision making. The most famous example was the Dred Scott case, which declared slavery constitutional. Five of the nine Supreme Court justices deciding the 1857 Dred Scott case were from southern states, including the chief justice and author of the decision, Roger Taney.

In the aftermath of the Civil War and particularly during the twentieth century, the importance of region in presidential consid-eration declined. Although more than half of the justices who served on the bench before the Civil War were Southerners, fewer than one-fourth of the justices in the twentieth century were from southern states. Yet, in 1937, Franklin Roosevelt nominated Senator Hugo Black of Alabama because the judicial circuit where he was from was not already represented on the Court.[38]

However, a new criterion, at least for some nomination processes, appeared—religion. President Woodrow Wilson appointed the first Jewish justice, Louis Brandeis, in 1916. Wilson's selection of Brandeis created the Jewish seat on the Court, which presidents until Richard Nixon continued. The "Jewish seat" lasted for more than 50 years with the appointment of Brandeis, followed by Felix Frankfurter and then Abe Fortas.[39]

Similarly, a "Catholic seat" became a feature of Court appoint-ments for more than 50 years. When the seat went vacant for several years, Catholics lobbied President Dwight Eisenhower to nominate a Catholic to the Court. Facing a vacancy only two months away from election day and eager to capture the Catholic vote, Eisenhower instructed his staff to find a Catholic candidate for the vacancy.[40] His pick, William Brennan, won quick confirmation and served on the Court for 34 years. Eisenhower won reelection and increased his share of the Catholic vote by 5 percent.[41]

For the most part, however, these designations of region and reli-gion have become less salient, even to the affected groups. Regional background plays little role today since all regions of the country have been represented on the Court at some time and regional differences are smaller than 200 years ago. In fact, President Clinton twice seriously considered nominating Interior Secretary Bruce Babbitt for the court even though, had he been confirmed, he would have been the third Arizonian on the bench.

Religion has also had little bearing on the selection process in recent years. The Jewish seat was left unfilled for 23 years. The fact that both Ruth Bader Ginsburg and Stephen Breyer were Jewish had little or no significance in the decision making of the Clinton administration.[42] Currently, three Catholics and two Jews sit on the Court, and the designation of such seats no longer exists. Although several religious groups, such as the Church of Jesus Christ of Latter-Day Saints (Mormons), Pentecostals, Muslims, and Orthodox, have never been represented on the Court, religious affiliation is not a significant factor in representativeness any longer.

Representativeness, however, has not disappeared as an aspect of presidential selection. Rather, it has been transformed into preoccupation with other demographic categories, particularly race, ethnicity, and gender. These have become the new measures of diversity for public officials, including Supreme Court justices.

Demographic representation or "diversity" has been urged by the press during presidential selection processes. For example, in 1993, the New York Times chided President Clinton for not searching more diligently for a nominee who was Jewish, black, or female.[43]

And that emphasis has been furthered by pressure from various interest groups representing social forces that have connected diversity to party support. The Supreme Court appointment process is part of that calculation. Laurence Tribe's view that the goal of racial and gender diversity is "a legitimate value" in the tradition of assignments of various seats has been widely accepted, whether for moral or strictly political reasons.[44]

Therefore, presidents have responded by attaching greater importance in the selection process to these demands for diversity. One example is candidate Ronald Reagan's pledge in 1980 to nominate a woman to one of the first vacancies on the Court. Another is Reagan's subsequent nomination of the first Italian American (Antonin Scalia). Successor George H. W. Bush also reacted to these expectations by giving overriding importance to race in the selection of a successor to Justice Thurgood Marshall in 1990.[45]

As a result, an African American seat now exists on the Court. George H. W. Bush was the first to continue the seat by appointing Clarence Thomas to succeed Marshall in 1991. However, the existence of such a seat was apparent, practically as soon as Marshall joined the Court. Even though Marshall had been a justice for only four years, Richard Nixon told his advisors to plan ahead if Marshall resigned during Nixon's term: "Let's be thinking of that black seat though, in case it comes up, because that's going to be one that you got to go to a black."[46]

President Clinton also felt such pressure from several directions when women's groups urged him to appoint a second female justice while Hispanics lobbied for one of their own to fill the vacancy. When Clinton announced the appointment of a non-Hispanic in 1994, White House Counsel Lloyd Cutler simultaneously revealed that the president would appoint Jose Cabranes to a federal appellate court opening in order to appease Hispanic groups concerned that the administration once again was ignoring their pleas. The implication was that Clinton might appoint Cabranes to the Supreme Court if another vacancy occurred during his presidency.

Race was first introduced as a selection factor when President Johnson tapped Thurgood Marshall for the Court in 1967. Segregationists such as Senator Strom Thurmond of South Carolina and Senator James Eastland of Mississippi vigorously fought the nomination, but Senate confirmation and changed societal attitudes on race relations presaged that Marshall's tenure would not be a one-time occurrence. African American representation would be a standard expectation on the Court.

Ethnicity has emerged in full force in the selection process as Hispanic groups have pressured recent presidents for representation on the Court. Twelve percent of Americans are of Hispanic origin; however, only since the George H. W. Bush administration have Hispanic candidates received serious consideration from presidents in the selection process. The George W. Bush administration received similar pressure from Hispanic groups to make the first appointment of a Hispanic justice. Hispanic groups recommended their own preferred candidates, but the most prominent Hispanic candidate from the White House's perspective was Alberto Gonzales, White House counsel.

Ethnicity as a factor in presidential consideration is not likely to fade soon. Instead, pressure may emanate from still more unrepresented groups, such as Asian groups or Native Americans, to place their candidates on the Court as well. However, their success may well depend on their ability to deliver significant electoral and party support in contested states.

Gender has acquired presidential attention as well, particularly since the women's movement in the early 1970s. In fact, lobbying for a woman Supreme Court justice began long before candidate Reagan's promise in 1980 to appoint a woman to one of the first vacancies on the Court. Both President Nixon and President Ford announced that women were on their short lists for consideration in the early and mid-1970s. President Ford's wife even publicly expressed her support for Carla Hills, a member of Ford's cabinet.[47] Changing societal attitudes about the role of women had increased public acceptance of the idea of a woman serving on the U.S. Supreme Court.[48]

Unlike other groups, women's organizations have asserted that a token seat is not enough. Arguing that they represent the majority of the population, women's groups have argued for more female members of the Court. That pressure became particularly intense during the Clinton administration. Leaders of women's groups believed Clinton was sympathetic with their interests. Their success in achieving a first-ever female head of the Justice Department signaled that the administration was prone to support their interests, and President Clinton's appointment of the second female justice responded to that pressure.

Representativeness is a critical factor in presidential selection that presidents cannot safely ignore. This is true particularly when the demands for representation from various groups may affect electoral politics. One example was the confirmation battle over the federal appellate nomination of Miguel Estrada, which Republicans hoped to use as a measure of the party's appeal to Hispanics in the 2004 presidential campaign.

Although this factor may appear to bind presidents, it may shelter them as well. Presidents can use this factor to gain nearly automatic support for a nominee from selected groups—women's groups for a female candidate or Hispanic groups for a Hispanic. In 1991, African American groups normally would have opposed any appointment by President Bush. However, Thomas's nomination divided blacks and weakened civil rights groups' opposition to confirmation.[49]

Yet, representativeness is still sublimated to other factors, particularly ideology. President George H. W. Bush appointed a conservative African American, while President Clinton selected a moderately liberal female nominee. Representativeness is rarely the end but the means.

Creating Vacancies

Obviously, these selection criteria are meaningless unless a vacancy actually exists. The fact that a vacancy is a prerequisite for presidential action is no small matter. The good fortune of a president in having a vacancy to fill has varied considerably from William Howard Taft's six appointments in one four-year term to Jimmy Carter's none during a similar period nearly 70 years later. Historically, vacancies have occurred about once every two years. Yet, following the appointment of Stephen Breyer in 1994, more than a decade passed until the next vacancy. That constituted the longest period of stability since early in the nineteenth century.

When a president sympathetic to their interests holds office, ideological groups nearly chomp at the bit for a Supreme Court retirement, particularly by a justice perceived as supportive of the groups' views, in order to offer the president the opportunity to appoint a new ideological confederate to the bench. For example, in the wake of the Court's decision to strike down antisodomy legislation in 2003, Pat Robertson, head of the Christian Broadcasting Network, urged his supporters to pray to encourage three more liberal justices to feel the need to retire: "Would it not be possible for God to put it in the minds of these three judges that the time has come to retire? With their retirement and the appointment of conservative judges, a massive change in federal jurisprudence can take place."[50]

Presidents have occasionally attempted to create a vacancy by removing a sitting justice. Most have been unsuccessful. Thomas Jefferson's partisan supporters in the Senate attempted to remove Samuel Chase in 1803 to provide Jefferson with another appointment.[51] Similarly, in 1970 the Nixon White House recruited House Minority Leader Gerald Ford to instigate impeachment proceedings against Justice William O. Douglas. Simultaneously, the Justice Department used the IRS to review Douglas's tax records and the FBI to wiretap Douglas's telephone conversations. The effort fizzled when nothing constituting an impeachable offense could be found against Douglas.[52]

Franklin Roosevelt's unsuccessful 1937 "court-packing plan" is the most famous such attempt to open new vacancies for the president to shape the Court.[53] Roosevelt's plan, which would have allowed the president to appoint one justice for every current justice over the age of 70, would have granted Roosevelt an opportunity to swiftly restructure the Court. As fate would have it, throughout his slightly more than 12 years in office Roosevelt ended up filling as many vacancies as he would have, had the court-packing plan passed.

However, other attempts actually have worked. After hearing rumors of a financial relationship between Justice Fortas and a convicted financier and leaking that news to *Life* magazine, Nixon "cleared his desk of other work to focus on getting Fortas off the Court."[54] Nixon's attorney general, John Mitchell, pressured Chief Justice Earl Warren to encourage Fortas to resign by threatening a messy criminal investigation of a sitting justice if Fortas remained. According to former White House Counsel John W. Dean, the Justice Department did not have enough evidence to convict Fortas, but, lacking support from his colleagues, Fortas resigned anyway.[55]

Lyndon Johnson was the master at creating vacancies. In 1965, Johnson strong-armed Arthur Goldberg from his life-tenure post on the Court to one as U.S. permanent representative to the United Nations, suggesting that Goldberg, who sought world peace, could do more for that cause in the latter post. Then, two years later, Johnson created a conflict of interest for Justice Tom C. Clark by appointing Clark's son, Ramsey Clark, as U.S. Attorney General. Since a large proportion of the cases the justices hear involve the U.S. government as a party, the appointment created a potential conflict of interest for Clark, who would be judging many cases prepared by (or even argued by) his son. As Johnson predicted, Clark decided to retire, which created another vacancy for Johnson to fill.[56]

Other Administration Players

The president has the final decision-making power in Supreme Court selection. However, the president is hardly the only administration player in selection politics. Others within the administration play critical roles in vetting candidates, creating short lists for presidential perusal, advising the president on political factors relative to an appointment, and shaping the timetable and even the outcome of presidential selection.

Sometimes presidents do make unilateral choices, even in advance of a vacancy. These choices may even be communicated to the prospective nominee. For example, President Franklin Roosevelt had promised his first Supreme Court appointment to Senate Majority Leader Joseph T. Robinson. However, Robinson's sudden fatal heart attack in the midst of the presidential selection process opened the process to others.[57] President Dwight Eisenhower also promised a Supreme Court appointment to an individual even before a vacancy had occurred. In his case, it was to California Governor Earl Warren.[58] In other cases, the favored person may not have a verbal assurance but still holds a strong presumption of appointment. When Justice Lewis Powell announced his retirement in 1987, Judge Robert Bork, the second choice the previous year, was the presumptive nominee for the Reagan administration.[59]

However, usually there is no presumptive choice. Rather, the process is open, with the outcome uncertain and ultimately shaped by the players—including not only the president but also those surrounding him.

Once a vacancy occurs and the process of nominating a candidate commences, how a president makes the decision significantly affects the outcome. Although presidents can make unilateral choices without even conferring with their staff, in reality modern presidents make the selection a quasi-collegial decision-making process. That *quasi* means that paring down candidates is a joint endeavor but that the president still retains final say over the outcome. The task of identifying, investigating, and evaluating candidates falls to a handful of presidential advisors.

Indeed, under certain circumstances these advisors may play expanded roles. One such situation is a president who possesses little interest in the Supreme Court or lacks a legal background. For example, President Ford relied heavily on his attorney general, Edward Levi, and the eventual nominee was a close associate of Levi's, John Paul Stevens. Ford did not consider himself an expert in constitutional law, even though he had a legal background as a graduate of Yale Law School and as an attorney. Three recent presidents—Ronald Reagan, George H. W. Bush, and George W. Bush—lacked even that experience.[60]

For some appointments, such presidents essentially have deferred to advisors. President Reagan had never heard of Sandra Day O'Connor before her nomination and had only one brief meeting with her before the nomination announcement. President George H. W. Bush learned of former New Hampshire Supreme Court judge David Souter through his chief of staff, John Sununu. Sununu knew Souter from the former's term as governor of New Hampshire.[61]

However, such advisors still operate within broadly defined presidential criteria. Reagan had promised that one of his first appointments to the Court would be a woman, thus limiting the pool of eligible applicants. Moreover, Reagan's appointment needed to be perceived as a conservative who would be acceptable to his core constituency—right-wing Republicans. Similarly, the Souter appointment came in the post-Bork environment, which demanded a stealth candidate who was considered reliably but unobtrusively conservative.

Presidents can set the criteria for staff selection lists. President Clinton told his aides: "Find me somebody who when the name is heard, people say, 'Yes. Wow. A home run. That person belongs on the Supreme Court.'"[62] Twenty years earlier, Richard Nixon told his attorney general, John Mitchell, that "our first requirement is . . . a southerner. The second requirement, he must be a conservative southerner."[63]

Some presidents monopolize the decision-making process. In those cases, presidents either know potential nominees personally or believe they have a command over the factors of presidential selection themselves. One example of the former is President Harry Truman, who appointed only people he knew well and considered friends. An example of the latter is President Bill Clinton. Unlike recent predecessors, Clinton possessed an uncommon interest in the process. Clinton not only was a graduate of Yale Law School but also had taught constitutional law at the University of Arkansas Law School. Moreover, First Lady Hillary Clinton was an attorney with her own expertise in the area of children's rights. The centralization of the decision-making process into his own hands was the result of his own perceived expertise. Even more extreme, Franklin Roosevelt offered the nomination to Senator Hugo Black before he even alerted any of his staff to his decision.[64]

Although the chief advisors in this process are usually the attorney general and top White House staff, the decision-making process may be more fluid. Determining who gets to participate rests primarily with the president. No set cast of players exists. President Clinton, for example, relied heavily on White House Counsel Bernard Nussbaum and left Attorney General Janet Reno "out of the loop" for two reasons: She was appointed late, and power already had been centralized in the White House. However, Richard Nixon reversed that relation-ship—leaning on Mitchell but rarely involving his own White House counsel, John Dean.[65]

Moreover, others may enter the process. For example, Hillary Clin-ton was widely perceived as influential in the selection process during her husband's administration because of her legal background and her involvement in other issues in the Clinton administration. The specu-lation appeared to be confirmed given the outcome, a female judge strongly identified with women's rights. Yet, if the first lady actually influenced the decision, she was effective in keeping her involvement hidden from public view.

Even those outside the Justice Department or the White House may seek to influence the president's choice. During the Nixon admin-istration, Nixon's transportation secretary, John Volpe, lobbied Nixon constantly to appoint an Italian American to the Court. Nixon desper-ately tried to do so and even considered appointing a woman with an Italian husband. Ultimately, Nixon chose someone else.[66]

Presidential advisors are not just minions in the process. They often represent factional views the president must arbitrate to reach a decision on a nominee.[67] For example, President Reagan's advisors included those who sought strongly conservative nominees such as Robert Bork or Douglas Ginsburg, as well as others who favored more moderate conservatives who would win easy confirmation.

Players beyond the Administration

Other players external to the administration also have acquired a mea-sure of importance in the selection process, depending on the open-ness of the president and on the political climate. The composition of the Senate, which shapes the body's attitude toward a nominee, affects presidential decision making. This will be discussed shortly. But indi-vidual senators can play a more direct role by encouraging the presi-dent to nominate certain individuals who, senators predict, will enjoy positive confirmation hearings and eventual successful votes. In 1993, a bipartisan coalition of members of the Senate Judiciary Committee expressed support for U.S. Circuit Court of Appeals Judge Stephen Breyer, a former counsel for the committee, to fill the vacancy left by Byron White.[68] Clinton bypassed Breyer in 1993 but returned to him for the nomination the next year.

Senators frequently suggest nominees from their own states or with whom they are close. Senator Warren Rudman of New Hampshire was a strong advocate for New Hampshire Judge David Souter's selection, and Senator John Danforth of Missouri played a comparable role for Clarence Thomas, who once served as Danforth's legislative aide. Both senators later became mentors for their respective candidates during the confirmation process.[69]

Senators apparently have become more public about their role in the selection process. Even when no vacancy existed, Senator Charles Schumer of New York sent President George W. Bush a public list of possible nominees, including fellow Senator Arlen Specter of Pennsylvania.[70]

Senators also may attempt privately to warn a president away from a potential nominee. In 1987, Senate Democratic Party leaders advised Reagan White House officials that nominating Robert Bork would trigger a protracted and bitter confirmation fight.[71]

Rather than specify a certain nominee, however, senators may attempt to influence the traits considered for selection. After the Bork defeat and Ginsburg withdrawal in 1987, Senator Patrick Leahy, a member of the Senate Judiciary Committee, warned the president that if he did not select a "readily acceptable" nominee that Reagan would not get another chance to fill the Supreme Court vacancy during his term.[72] (Reagan nominated Anthony Kennedy, who was perceived as a more moderate conservative and easily won confirmation.) In 2003, the George W. Bush administration similarly was warned by Senator Schumer that the president should nominate someone the whole Senate could support rather than a nominee who could win the support of 51 Republican senators.[73]

The president also may choose to include senators in the decision-making process by soliciting their opinions. President Clinton asked for advice from various senators, including both Democrats such as Edward Kennedy and Daniel Patrick Moynihan and Republicans such as Bob Dole and Orrin Hatch. Yet, other presidents may exclude the Senate altogether. One senator remarked that he had no idea who Franklin Roosevelt would appoint for a vacancy because the "President certainly has not consulted anybody in the Senate about it."[74]

Another involved group outside the administration is the legal community. Prior to the 1970s, the ABA was accorded the opportunity to intervene even before the selection of a nominee. The organization's Standing Committee on Federal Judiciary provided an initial screening of potential presidential picks. However, as mentioned earlier, accusations of leaks resulted in subsequent exclusion.[75] Yet, the ABA's rating of nominees before a Senate confirmation vote, and the emphasis other players place on that rating, cannot help but affect presidential decision making today because no president wishes to have a nominee labeled unqualified, and even a "qualified" rating strengthens the position of the nominee's critics.

Other elements of the legal community—from national organizations to individual legal scholars—have weighed in on Supreme Court nominations during the presidential selection stage. These lobbying efforts take the form of letters and petitions to the president. The classic model is the successful effort by the legal community to encourage Herbert Hoover to nominate New York Court of Appeals Judge Benjamin Cardozo for a vacancy in 1932.[76]

A subset of the legal community with a special interest in the selection process includes the current justices. Sitting justices usually avoid public involvement in the selection process, but private involvement has been sought on occasion. John F. Kennedy solicited the justices' advice on an appointment in 1962.

On other occasions, unsolicited recommendations are offered. Historically, one of the most intrusive justices in the selection process was Chief Justice William Howard Taft, who played an active role in the judicial selection process in the Harding and Coolidge administrations.[77] Two justices urged President Truman to appoint Fred Vinson as chief justice in 1946, which he did.

Similarly, Chief Justice Warren Burger advised Republican presidents Nixon and Reagan on Court appointments.[78] Burger met with Nixon and his aides to discuss potential Supreme Court nominees and sent frequent letters to the Nixon White House in an attempt to direct the process in one way or another. For example, Burger strongly opposed Nixon appointing a woman to a vacancy in 1971, when Nixon seriously considered nominating Mildred Lillie, a California appellate court judge. Burger even went so far as threatening to resign from the Court if Nixon appointed a female justice.[79]

Occasionally, recent sitting justices have expressed public comments on nominees. Both Byron White and John Paul Stevens expressed support for Robert Bork's appointment in 1987, and Thurgood Marshall commented after David Souter's nomination that he had "never heard of him."[80]

Individuals and groups not involved in the process attempt to influence the outcome by lobbying the White House and/or "going public" with preferred nominees or preferred traits of a nominee. Usually the pressure comes from outside groups. The role of these outside players depends partly on the speed with which the president makes a decision. If the period between the announcement of a vacancy and the nomination of a replacement is lengthy, outside groups possess the time to lobby privately and pressure publicly. However, presidents who act quickly rob these groups of their opportunity to apply pressure before an announcement is made. For example, President George H. W. Bush chose a replacement for William Brennan three days after Brennan retired.[81]

At times, retiring justices have aided the administration in privatizing the process. Chief Justice Warren Burger offered the Reagan administration the opportunity to conduct the selection process in secret when he privately informed the president three months before the public announcement of his retirement, which also included Burger's designated successor as chief justice, William Rehnquist, as well as his replacement on the Court, Antonin Scalia. In 1971, Justice John Harlan II allowed the White House to dictate the timing of his retirement announcement. Nixon was grateful and remarked privately that "my judgment on the announcement thing was the longer you could keep it, right within your own bosom, the more you keep your options open."[82] However, presidents often do not have the luxury of such a closed process.

The rapidity with which a president makes decisions also hinges on the amount of time the retiring justice gives the president to appoint a new successor before the next term of the Court begins on the first Monday in October. Presidents Reagan and George H. W. Bush were notified of vacancies in June or July. In the case of Clarence Thomas, because Anita Hill's accusations prompted a new round of committee testimony, the confirmation stage extended into the Court's next term. When justices announce their retirement at the end of the Court's term, which has been the common practice for several recent justices, the president has a brief time to consider the possibilities, name a nominee, and then seek to win Senate confirmation, before the new justice needs to start work. The length of the confirmation stage, including Senate background investigation and hearings schedules, interrupted by a month-long August recess, truncates the time the president is allowed for the selection stage.

Mindful of the president's dilemma, in 1993 and 1994 retiring justices announced their departures in March and April, respectively, in order to grant the president more time to consider candidates and get a nominee confirmed by the Senate. Ironically, in 1993 Justice Byron White's early announcement did little good in extending the confirmation stage because President Clinton took three months to name a successor.

Aware of the rapidity with which choices may be made, particularly when justices announce retirements at the end of the term, groups with ties to the White House (such as conservative groups in the Reagan and two Bush administrations or liberals during the Clinton administration) organize lists of nominees for presidential consideration in anticipation of a selection. In some cases, such as the George W. Bush administration, groups had many months to develop lists, conduct research on potential nominees, and signal privately and even publicly group opinions for or against possible candidates.

Presidential Management: Constituency or Consensus

Next is the president's role in the preparation for the next stage of the process—Senate deliberations and the ultimate vote on the nominee. The president's management of a nomination, even in the selection stage, clearly affects confirmation chances. According to John Massaro, the president is responsible for overseeing a strategy that results in eventual confirmation. Part of this presidential management process is selecting a confirmable nominee while still maintaining the president's goal of influencing the ideological direction of the Court.[83] Presidents do not want nominees who cannot be confirmed and thus embarrass the president. President Nixon wanted his legislative staff to commit senators even before announcing his selection.[84]

The White House determines how nominees will be "sold" to the Senate. Successful presidential management begins at the nomination stage, as the White House determines which of the candidates for the nomination can win a majority of the Senate. The White House assesses confirmation chances in discussions with interest groups who can offer potential endorsements and grassroots support. In addition, members of the Senate who seek to influence the president's decision can alert the president to the breadth of potential support for a nominee within the chamber.

Presidential management is more than the decision about candidate selection, however. It includes creation of a strategy capable of ultimately winning confirmation support. In approaching nominee selection, presidents survey the political environment and adopt either a constituency approach or a consensual approach.

Constituency Model

The constituency method gratifies the expectations of the president's core constituency. It can be the most satisfying for a president in several ways. It appeases groups who provided early and intense electoral support for the president and offer the greatest support in a crisis situation. And it produces a nominee closest to the ideology of the president. The constituency approach in the post-Bork era of Supreme Court nominations, by which groups adopt slash-and-burn tactics in supporting or opposing nominees, offers constituencies a battle to join where victory is sweet because it includes overwhelming defeat of the opposing side. After a successful, albeit bitter, confirmation fight, groups can take satisfaction that a justice will sit on the Court who clearly reflects the constituency's ideological perspective and may even lead the Court over years of policy making in a direction favorable to the constituency groups.

Those closest to the president—constituency groups, senators from the president's party, and even advisors who represent that faction within the party—may be those advocating the constituency approach. If the president's party controls the Senate, they may argue vehemently, relying on the premise that a positive vote for a controversial nominee is almost assured.

The constituency approach promises a pitched battle over the nominee. The nominee may win, but only after a protracted, bloody conflict between the two parties and their supporters. The final vote will be close or at least include significant opposition. However, again, if the Senate is in the hands of the president's party, particularly if it is firmly in those hands (filibuster-proof), theoretically a constituency choice is confirmable. The Reagan administration, in its nomination of Judge Robert Bork, appeared to be choosing this option by selecting a nominee certain to lose the support of many Democrats, but closer to the ideological leanings of the president and constituent interest groups. Other recent constituency choices included William Rehnquist and Clarence Thomas.

But the constituency approach is highly risky. Opposition forces may successfully mobilize to cast doubt on the ability of the nominee to be confirmed. Even when the president's party controls the Senate, if it is a narrow majority, the opposition may be able to pull enough majority party senators to the opposition side to defeat the nomination. And if the president's party does not control the chamber, the constituency approach may promise an uphill battle for confirmation. Confirmation failure is the likely outcome. Not surprisingly, constituency choices such as Douglas Ginsburg (Reagan) and Abe Fortas (Johnson) have been those most likely to be withdrawn in the face of certain defeat. Others have gone down to defeat, such as Bork, Haynsworth, and Carswell.

Consensual Model

The second approach is the consensual model. Here the president finds a nominee who appeals across party lines—a moderate who is palatable to both liberal and conservative groups. President Clinton took this approach when choosing his two nominees—Ruth Bader Ginsburg and Stephen Breyer. Both received minimal opposition in the Senate. Other consensual choices included John Paul Stevens, Sandra Day O'Connor, and Anthony Kennedy—all of whom were opposed by only a small minority of senators or by none at all. Antonin Scalia was a constituency choice, but opposition forces spent their resources in an unsuccessful fight against Rehnquist's confirmation as chief justice and acquiesced when faced with Democratic senators who were unwilling to wage another confirmation battle on the heels of one they had just lost.

Presidents enjoy the praise they get when they appoint candidates highly regarded within the legal community. Clinton's search for a collective "wow" from others is an example. Nixon at one point in his presidency contemplated appointing a Yale law school professor and remarked to his staff that "everybody would say, well, we finally appointed a scholar. I'd love that."[85]

The consensual approach would seem the logical one from the standpoint of winning confirmation. But a president faces enormous pressures from constituent groups to adopt the constituency approach. Moreover, when spurned after such appeals, these same groups may punish the president by withdrawing crucial support.

The determination of approach may rest with several factors. One is the personality of the president. A president with a strong ideological approach may see the constituency model as merely his duty to tilt the Court toward his philosophy. But another factor is the timing of a vacancy. A president who faces a pending reelection campaign may move toward the constituency approach to satisfy constituent groups on whom he must rely for reelection. President George H. W. Bush apparently took that approach in 1991 when he nominated Clarence Thomas. Moreover, Bush had never been popular with the most conservative wing of the Republican Party. That example points to another environment factor: The president may be more likely to respond to constituent group demands if he is not perceived as firmly in their camp and needs to curry favor with the core constituency of his party.

When the constituency approach is used, presidents face the decision of the extent to which the battle is joined. For example, the Nixon administration launched a direct mail campaign to 30,000 publications to gain press support for one nominee and, in another case, orchestrated a letters-to-the-editor campaign in which professionals wrote letters signed and submitted by Republican loyalists to newspapers around the nation.[86] Presidents themselves have acquired an increasingly public role in supporting their nominees during the confirmation process.[87]

Yet, they have varied in their approach to nominees in trouble. Ronald Reagan was the first president to personally support his troubled Supreme Court nominee in public with his strong initial backing for Robert Bork.[88] However, later in the process the Reagan White House backed away from Robert Bork and Douglas Ginsburg when each nominee encountered difficulty in the confirmation process.[89] President Bush, on the other hand, continued to support Thomas even after the Anita Hill accusations by lobbying for Thomas up to the final vote of 52-48 in the Senate.[90]

The Confirmation

There are no constitutional guidelines on the role of the Senate in judicial nominations. The Senate itself has adopted its own rules—both formal and informal—to govern the process. Even the adoption of those rules was gradual in nature. The full-blown Senate Judiciary

Committee hearings and floor debate are fairly recent developments in the process. For example, until 1929, the Senate debated Supreme Court nominations in private. The Judiciary Committee's role was minimal. Hearings in committee were held sporadically.[91]

Even when hearings existed, they were not routinely exhaustive, as they are today. Some were, but many were perfunctory meetings where senators quickly voted to accept a nominee. For example, Felix Frankfurter, a Franklin Roosevelt appointee, appeared before the Senate Judiciary Committee and was confirmed by the full Senate a mere 12 days after Roosevelt announced his nomination.[92]

The role of the nominee in the confirmation process evolved slowly as well. Until 1925, nominees themselves did not testify at those hearings.[93] Some were never requested to testify or were not allowed to do so.[94] Others refused on the grounds that it was inappropriate. In 1949, Sherman Minton became the last nominee to decline to appear when requested. William Rehnquist wanted to take the same stand when he was nominated as chief justice in 1986. Initially, Rehnquist felt it was inappropriate for a sitting justice to endure such questioning, but the climate in the Senate had changed substantially since the 1940s. No longer would the Senate tolerate the refusal of a nominee to appear. Ultimately, the White House dissuaded him from taking that recalcitrant position, and Rehnquist testified like any other nominee for confirmation.[95]

However, the most significant formal rule today is the delegation of responsibility for the screening of nominees to the Judiciary Committee. The Judiciary Committee has adopted a tradition of making a recommendation to the full Senate only after holding formal and exhaustive hearings.

Allocation of power to a committee became the nexus of controversy during the Thomas nomination. After sexual harassment charges were raised by University of Oklahoma law professor Anita Hill, a proposal was debated to allow senators not on the Judiciary Committee to question Thomas and Hill. The Senate's final resolution in favor of the committee's exclusive jurisdiction reinforced the salience of that group in the Senate's deliberative process.

An informal rule is senatorial courtesy—the Senate's policy of deferring to the will of the senators, particularly those of the president's party, who come from the same state as the nominee. Senatorial courtesy is much stronger at lower federal judicial appointments, but it has surfaced at the Supreme Court level occasionally. Two of Grover Cleveland's nominees (both from New York) were rejected because of the active opposition of a senator from the nominees' home state.[96]

The Senate has usually provided its consent to Supreme Court nominations. However, this record of support belies the existence of political factors determining whether a president's choice ultimately will sit on the nation's highest bench. Four major factors predict the Senate's response to a presidential nominee: institutional jealousy, partisanship and ideology, timing of the appointment, and the nature of the specific nominee.

Institutional Jealousy

Fighting over confirmation is often portrayed as a partisan war. However, it is more than that. As Jeffrey Segal notes, "The battle is not just between Republicans and Democrats, but between the Senate and the president."[97] The most dangerous condition for confirmation of the president's selection is institutional animosity between the White House and the Congress. In an era of jealousy between the Congress and the president, presidents find Senate consent of Supreme Court nominations problematic because the Senate does not wish to appear acquiescent to the president.

Today is one of those periods. The Senate now is more prone to challenge a judicial nomination than it was 40 years ago. As a result of that institutional jealousy, as Henry J. Abraham notes, the Senate "may be second therein but it is not secondary."[98]

Since the late 1960s, Congress has sought a more aggressive posture in protecting its powers vis-à-vis the executive, particularly in the areas of foreign policy and the budget.[99] Divided government—that is, control of the White House by one party and control of the

Senate by the other—has enhanced institutional jealousy, a point that will be discussed later.

The appointment power in areas outside the judicial branch also has been affected. Traditionally, under the theory that the president, not the Senate, should choose those who will serve in the executive branch, almost all executive appointments have been confirmed. But more recently the Senate's assertiveness has led to even some of those nonjudicial appointments being rejected by formal vote or withdrawn in anticipation of rejection.[100]

Supreme Court appointments, on the other hand, have acquired their own special status because of the president's intent to influence Court direction through personnel changes. The president is seeking to reach beyond the executive branch and even beyond the president's term in office to shape public policy. The success of a nomination in a period of Senate acquiescence to presidential initiatives is more

Table 2.1

Time Period between Nomination and Confirmation of Supreme Court Justices

Dates	Number of Justices Confirmed	Average # of Days Per Justice
1789–1809	16	2.56
1810–1830	6	8
1831–1850	9	11.56
1851–1870	10	12.3
1871–1890	11	24.91
1891–1910	12	8.33
1911–1930	10	24.1
1931–1950	13	12.62
1951–1970	11	57.91
1971–1980	3	38.6
1981–1990	5	94.3
1991–1994	3	75.7

Source: Powell–Kennedy, *Congressional Quarterly's Guide to the Supreme Court*, second edition, 1990, appendix, p. 998.
Souter–Breyer, *Congressional Quarterly's Guide to the Supreme Court*, "Listing of Justices Biography," January 28, 1995.

Table 2.2
Number of Days Elapsed between Nomination and Confirmation
for Supreme Court Nominees 1971–1994

	1970s	1980s	1990s
Lewis F. Powell Jr.	46		
William H. Rehnquist	50		
John Paul Stevens	20		
Sandra Day O'Connor		107	
William H. Rehnquist		92	
Antonin Scalia		92	
Robert Bork		115	
Anthony Kennedy		65	
David Souter			69
Clarence Thomas			107
Ruth Bader Ginsberg			50
Stephen Breyer			77
Decade Average*	39	94	76

*Rounded to the nearest full day.

predictable than during one of legislative branch assertiveness. But recent presidents, confronted with institutional jealousy, have a more difficult task of acquiring Senate confirmation.

Even the task of confirmation has become a more elongated process. Whereas in an earlier era confirmations occurred within days, sometimes even within hours of a presidential nomination, today the confirmation process stretches over months. (See Table 2.1.)

The growth in the length of the confirmation period has been most pronounced in the last quarter century. Table 2.2 shows the increase in the length of that period for nominations between 1971 and 1994. The average length of the period was only 39 days in the 1970s. It increased to 94 days in the 1980s, which included several lengthy processes. The Robert Bork process alone was longer than all the 1970s confirmations put together. Even the briefer Anthony Kennedy confirmation process in 1987–1988 significantly outlasted those in the 1970s.

Table 2.3
Average Number of Days between Nomination and Confirmation
by Party Control of Senate and White House

Party Control	1970s	1980s	1990s
Same-party control		97	64
Split-party control	39	90	88

Table 2.3 shows that the increase in the 1980s was true both when the Senate and the White House were dominated by the same party and when they were not. The 1990s nominations are more distinctive from each other in their differences. Same-party control resulted in shorter processes, but that was still nearly double the length of the process under split-party control in the 1970s. The nomination process is clearly longer, no matter which party controls the Senate or whether any significant opposition is attached to the nomination.

Partisanship and Ideology

A key determinant in the outcome of the process has been the partisan affiliation of the president and a majority of the Senate. Historically, nominations have been more successful when the president and the Senate majority share party ties. A 1986 study found 89 percent of nominees had been confirmed when the president's party held a Senate majority, whereas 59 percent were confirmed when it did not.[101] Of the six nominees rejected by the Senate or withdrawn from consideration in the past half century, four faced Senate majorities controlled by the opposition party.[102]

Partisanship includes ideology and relationship to the president. Senators of the president's party not only are more likely to share the ideological leanings of the nominee, and therefore favor confirmation, but also are interested in offering support for the president's initiatives. Conversely, those of the opposition party are less likely to agree with a nominee who shares the president's legal philosophy and, on political grounds, have little stake in seeing the president succeed in reshaping the Court in the opposite direction.

Yet, even when the opposing party has controlled the Senate, the philosophy of allowing the president to choose a justice in line with his views long prevailed. As recently as the 1970s, two political scientists concluded that "senators expect and normally grant to the President the right to appoint to the Court men who share the President's own political philosophy."[103]

Since the Robert Bork nomination, whether the ideological leanings of the nominee should be addressed has become the crux of a Senate debate.[104] Recent nominations have included questions about the nominee's views on various issues. Although Sandra Day O'Connor received less criticism when choosing which of her views on issues to express, today's nominees are not allowed such latitude.[105]

However, the question of the Senate's role in examining the candidates' views is hardly new. When Judge Parker was defeated in 1930, this issue surfaced.[106] According to Robert F. Nagel, the Senate accepted the propriety of the practice as early as 1959, when the committee quizzed nominee Potter Stewart on specific cases, judicial philosophy, and his attitudes toward issues.[107]

Whether ideology is an open factor is almost a moot point because it has long served as at least a covert one. Senators have accepted an overt discussion of ideology as an important factor in the Senate's deliberation of nominees, although one study concluded that its salience depends on the nominee's legal qualifications and the general political environment.[108] Yet, as will be seen later, the overt nature of ideology in the process has affected the role of external forces as well.

Timing

Presidents cannot control the creation of a vacancy (although some have attempted to influence it); nevertheless, they are affected by its timing. For a lame duck president or one facing a difficult reelection, filling a vacancy on the Court is highly problematic. A vacancy that occurs during the president's final year is the least likely to result in a successful confirmation.[109] Senators of the opposition party believe they can outlast the president and, if their party wins the presidency, achieve a more favorable nominee.

The president's prime moment is when public support is high, the president carries a reservoir of political capital to expend on a controversial nominee, and the Senate is keenly aware of the president's strength. Conversely, a president politically weakened by other factors (such as low public approval ratings, the failure to win a high-profile appointment, or defeat on a key legislative vote) is in much greater danger of facing Senate opposition.

Through most of his term, for example, President Reagan was successful in making appointments to the Court. But following the Iran-contra affair, which diminished the perception of presidential invincibility, the Senate felt freer to oppose his choices. Senate assertiveness contributed to the administration's failure with two of its three nominees during his last two years in office.

Two other examples of presidential weakness when entering a Supreme Court selection process were Gerald Ford and Bill Clinton. Ford was an unelected president who followed on the heels of the Watergate scandal. He desperately wanted to win election in 1976. Therefore, he sought an uncontroversial appointment that would burnish his credentials for integrity while not offending either Democratic senators or the right wing of the Republican Party, which wanted a more aggressive and well-known conservative.[110] Similarly, Bill Clinton faced tepid public support, even in his first few months in office, and conservatives promised a tough fight over any Supreme Court nominee perceived as overtly liberal or politically astute.[111]

The confluence of events, many not even directly bearing on the president, can have an impact on the Senate's consideration of the nomination. For example, in an era of heightened discussion of sexual harassment, Anita Hill's charges against Clarence Thomas surfaced and nearly scuttled his confirmation. The charge probably would not have carried as much weight in a climate of societal disinterest in investigating such an accusation.

The Nominee

The background of the nominee and that person's behavior during the confirmation process are major factors in a successful outcome. The conventional wisdom is that a senator holds the best chances for success because the Senate rarely rejects one of its own for higher office. Harold Burton, a senator from Ohio, was unanimously confirmed by his colleagues when President Truman nominated him in 1945.[112] A chairman of the Senate Judiciary Committee during the Roosevelt presidency once suggested that the Senate had a tradition of forgoing committee investigation of a senator-nominee because "no amount of investigation or consideration by a committee could disclose any new light on the character or attainments and ability of the nominee, because if we do not know him after long service with the nominee no one will ever know him."[113]

Even a former Senate staff member can benefit from the Senate connection. In 1994, President Clinton nominated Stephen Breyer, a federal appellate judge who had formerly served as chief counsel of the Senate Judiciary Committee. As noted earlier, Breyer was supported by members of the committee from both parties.

Conversely, a nominee too closely associated with the president may have trouble. The presumption is that such an individual will become an extension of the Oval Office within a branch that cherishes the perception of independence.[114] When President Harry Truman nominated Attorney General Tom Clark for the Court in 1949, opponents charged Truman with cronyism because of Clark's long-time role as a campaigner for Truman. One opponent labeled Clark a "second-rate political hack" who was selected "as a result of raw political favoritism."[115] Confirmation stage behavior also shapes the Senate's response. Nominees no longer can afford to appear arrogant before the Senate Judiciary Committee. The nominee must appear cooperative with the Senate in its investigative function, which explains the Reagan administration's remonstrance with William Rehnquist that he not appear to be uncooperative toward senators. Members of the Senate Judiciary Committee no longer allow nominees to refuse to answer questions. Although the nominee's actual answer may not be any more illuminating than a non-answer, the act of open refusal is viewed as offensive to the committee.

3

How the Process Broke

The Transformation of the Supreme Court
Appointment Process

On July 1, 1987, President Ronald Reagan announced that his choice
to replace Justice Lewis Powell was Judge Robert Bork, a well-known
judge on the District of Columbia Court of Appeals and a former acting attorney general of the United States. Bork had long been the
favorite of conservatives, but his nomination by Reagan signaled that
the administration was willing to confront its opponents with a controversial nominee.

Opposition from a broad array of interest groups, negative coverage by the press, and a gradual slide in public opinion were the
characteristics of that nomination that dramatically separated it from
those before. Robert Bork Jr., the son of Robert Bork, concluded that
his father had been "caught in the politics of the media age in which
image becomes reality."[1] Suzanne Garment, a Bork supporter, wrote
that "there had never been anything remotely resembling the scale
of the national media campaign that was launched against Bork. Nor
was there ever anything like the degree to which constituency interest groups were organized to put sustained pressure on individual
senators."[2]

External forces were potent players in that process. A coalition of
more than 300 interest groups combined to defeat Bork.[3] Moreover,
a large national audience watched C-SPAN and CNN coverage of the
Senate Judiciary Committee hearings.

The Post-Bork Period

Unlike previous controversial nominations, the Bork nomination process did not become an isolated event. Again, in 1991, during the Thomas confirmation hearings, a Supreme Court nomination became caught in a web of extensive television coverage, interest group competition, and frequent resort to public opinion.

In the wake of the Bork and Thomas nominations, some analysts concluded that the nomination process had been changed irrevocably. Political scientist Gregory Caldiera concluded that, in Supreme Court nominations, "organized group mobilization and pressure has become a permanent feature of our political landscape."[4]

As we have seen, the Bork nomination was not the commencement of the transformation to a public Supreme Court nomination process. Nor were the changes in the process attributable only to the intense efforts of the interest groups making up the anti-Bork coalition. These groups certainly contributed to Bork's defeat, but they alone did not alter the process. The process was already undergoing change when the Bork nomination occurred.

But what has driven external forces to become permanent players, and why have traditional players acquiesced to, if not facilitated, such roles? One answer lies in the theory of the scope and bias of conflict.

Scope and Bias of Conflict

Political scientist E. E. Schattschneider proposed that as the scope of a political conflict is enlarged, its bias changes.[5] The motivation for expanding the scope of a conflict is a desire to win and an expectation that the expansion of the conflict's scope will produce victory for those who are losing in the narrower sphere of the existing conflict. Schattschneider did not apply his scope and bias of conflict theory specifically to the Supreme Court nomination process. However, this theory may help explain the expansion of the Supreme Court appointment process to external players.

In accordance with this theory, we would expect that if inside players in the Supreme Court nomination process were losing internally, they would expand the scope of the conflict to include hitherto uninvolved players. These players, then, would tip the balance of power in favor of the outcome desired by the elites who mobilized them. Then, once one side had mobilized external players supportive of their position, the opposing set of elites would be forced to do the same to remain competitive. Hence, the battle would be joined. The fact that external players have indeed become involved in successive nomination conflicts as never before suggests that this scenario is precisely what has occurred in Supreme Court nominations. How does this theory actually play out in the recent history of Supreme Court nominations? What would motivate inside players in Supreme Court nominations to expand the scope of conflict in recent years?

Motives for Inside Players

Because partisan control of the White House and Congress has rotated between the two major parties over the past half century, both sides periodically lost internally and therefore possessed sufficient motive to move the conflict to a broader scope where victory might be possible. We should expect such behavior to have occurred over the entire course of U.S. history and not just recently, but, with a few exceptions, it has not. What has happened more recently to create the incentives for enlarging the scope of Supreme Court nomination conflict?

Divided Government

The 2000 election created the most divided government in memory. The Democratic presidential candidate took the popular vote while the Republican took the electoral vote. The House of Representatives was split 221–212, and the Senate was evenly divided. Republicans gained control of the chamber by virtue of the tie-breaking vote of the vice president of the United States.

The excitement did not end there. Six months later, Senator James Jeffords of Vermont heightened the partisan tension by abandoning the Republicans and declaring himself an Independent. He promised to vote with the Democrats to reorganize the Senate. Then, the 2002 elections tipped Senate control back to the Republicans, although barely (51–48–1).

As Senate Republicans and Democrats switched party leader and committee chair roles for the fourth time in two years, partisanship reached all-time highs in the Senate. Tension boiled over in areas such as committee control, office space, and the movement of legislation.

The tensions raised by the seesaw nature of presidential and Senate control spilled over onto another branch—the judiciary. With Republican control of both the White House and the Senate, the White House finally could press presidential nominees through the Senate Judiciary Committee and the Senate as a whole. With a near majority and prospects of retaking the Senate, Democrats employed the filibuster to block some appellate judicial appointments and prepared to do so for a Supreme Court nomination as well.

As the 2000 election and recent periods of divided government demonstrate, control of the Senate by the opposition party offers an institutional power base for nomination opponents. That presence has become more frequent in the past half century. Over the course of U.S. history, including the first half of the twentieth century, divided government was uncommon. Presidents typically could rely on confirmation because of routine support from the vast majority of their own party members within the Senate. Single-party control of both the White House and the Senate enhances presidential prospects for confirmation, even of a constituency nominee. Members of the minority party know that the opposition faces an uphill battle when the majority controls both the process and the likely outcome.

During the past half century, however, divided government in American politics has become more routine than exceptional. What the French call "cohabitation"—opposition parties sharing responsibility for government—has become a regular feature of American national politics.

Divided government in the last half century has provided an opportunity for sustained, meaningful opposition to the president. Between 1952 and 1998, half of presidential and mid-term elections resulted in divided government between the president and the Senate. By comparison, in the first half of the twentieth century, only four elections resulted in divided control of government.[6] With the exception of Jimmy Carter, since 1969 all presidents have faced opposition party control of the Senate during at least part of their term.

The result has been greater conflict between these two branches over the issue of judicial appointments because opponents more frequently today hold leverage over the president's fortunes in filling the Court. With majority control, the critics of the appointment can be more effectively heard during the hearing process, debate, and final votes. A united opposition party can carry a vote to a negative conclusion or send a clear signal to a president to withdraw a nomination before it is subject to likely defeat.

Granted, the power to block action on a Supreme Court nomination long existed through filibuster. However, not until 1968 did opposition Senators use that threat to block a Supreme Court nomination. That threat was successful, leading President Johnson to withdraw Abe Fortas's nomination for chief justice. (Rule changes have made filibusters more difficult to sustain without broad minority support.) There is a drawback with the filibuster as a minority weapon. It can carry the image of obstructionism, which usually bears a strongly negative connotation in American politics.

Congressional Resurgence

A specific incentive for senators has been the assertion of congressional power vis-à-vis the presidency. In the mid-1880s, Woodrow Wilson, as a graduate student at Johns Hopkins University, wrote a dissertation, later published as *Congressional Government*.[7] Wilson's thesis was that U.S. government power rested in Congress, not the presidency. Policy leadership was the purview of the legislative body, and the presidency was a decidedly secondary branch to the dominant legislature.

But by the turn of the twentieth century, Wilson reversed himself. He wrote another book, *Constitutional Government in the United States*, arguing that power had shifted to the presidency.[8] Wilson himself later became president and sought to expand presidential powers further.

Nor was he alone in doing so. Franklin D. Roosevelt contributed to institutionalizing presidential power and the expectation of policy leadership, particularly in the first term. Lyndon Johnson used expanded presidential power to pass Great Society legislation and pursue the Vietnam War largely unchecked by the Congress.

By the end of the Johnson presidency and the beginning of the Nixon administration, however, the willingness of Congress to defer to the president was fraying. The Vietnam War and the Watergate scandal tarnished the credibility of the presidency and led to a resurgence of congressional power, as evidenced in legislative acts such as the Budget and Impoundment Act, which gave Congress more power over the budget-making process; the War Powers Act, which was intended to limit presidential war-making power; and the passage of Articles of Impeachment against a sitting president for only the second time in American history. (The first time had been during the era of congressional power Wilson wrote about.)

The Republican revolution of 1994–1995, resulting in GOP control of both houses of Congress for the first time in 40 years, was a seminal act in congressional reemergence. The 104th Congress briefly took over the policy agenda, while the president was relegated to a secondary role. Although the president later resurfaced as legislative leader, the second impeachment of a president in the nation's history again demonstrated Congress's willingness to act aggressively vis-à-vis a sitting president.

Congressional resurgence of power affected its relations with the president in areas of policy leadership—both foreign and domestic. However, it also spilled over into the nomination process. Whereas senators previously may have accepted deference to the president's appointment power over the judicial branch, the post-Vietnam, post-Watergate atmosphere led Congress to question the legitimacy of that approach.

The Senate's treatment of judicial nominations is a prime example. As discussed earlier, senators have become more aggressive in blocking even lower level federal judicial appointments.

Expectations of the Role of Justices

Another significant development is the anticipated role of the justices as policy makers. As the Court has acquired an expanded role as a policy arbiter in national politics, the institution has come under increased scrutiny as a policy-making institution. That scrutiny suggests the Court should be treated much like other policy-making institutions.

Societal mores increasingly have dictated that a variety of diverse groups should be represented at the table when policy is made. The creation of more minority districts and the election of more racial minorities such as Native Americans, African Americans, and Hispanics have been acclaimed as actions producing greater representation of the nation's diversity.

The court has not been immune to those forces. The Court increasingly has been viewed as a body that should represent the greater diversity in the American populace.[9] This expectation makes representativeness a potent force in presidential selection.

But the battle ensues over which group gets representation at which time, particularly on a bench where only nine individuals sit. Additionally, the life tenure of justices and the infrequent turnover on the Court heighten the expectations of elites—the president or opponents—to use an appointment as an opportunity to affect representation.

Motives of External Players

However, the scope and bias of conflict theory does not answer why external players would participate. Why would they, in turn, join in the conflict? They, too, must possess some incentives to participate. What are the motives of external players that lead them to contribute to processes best known for being distant and relatively closed fights?

Effects of Court's Policy-Making Role

One incentive is the direct effect Supreme Court decisions have on external players. By 1987, the year of the Robert Bork nomination, the Court's increased role in social policy issues of our time, such as abortion, school desegregation, affirmative action, and civil liberties, provoked a public debate about the Court's policy-making role.[10] The effect of Court decisions on ordinary citizens' lives, as well as group agendas, meant that the public and groups could not ignore the acts of the Court or the impact individual justices had on the shaping of those acts.

Not surprisingly, then, concern about these effects spilled over into the nomination process.[11] Recent presidents have used as a significant criterion in the selection process the potential justice's stance on that debate. For example, while a candidate in 1988, George H. W. Bush promised that he would appoint judges who would not be part of a "liberal majority."[12] Advocates of judicial restraint generally have held the advantage in choosing nominees because of the greater number of vacancies during Republican administrations. But opponents such as liberal, pro-choice, and women's groups have viewed such appointments as threats to their policy gains through litigation and have launched campaigns to counter Republican efforts to shape the Court.

Naturally, the Court's increased role has heightened interest in the nomination process. Groups affected by Court policy have a stake in the direction of the Court, which is determined, to a great degree, by its membership. William G. Ross explains that "active participation by such groups [in judicial selection] is inevitable as long as the Supreme Court continues to have such a profound impact upon the life of the nation."[13] Although presidents have long sought to appoint justices who reflect their views on the direction of public policy, the extension of the Court's role in the past half century increased the perceived necessity for various groups to affect the Court through its personnel. As Mark Silverstein has pointed out, "Powerful groups from all points along the judicial spectrum now consider a sympathetic judiciary essential to the development and achievement of important policy goals."[14]

Since ideology had become an acceptable public criterion for assessing the merit of a nominee, conservatives have sought to "pack" the Court with like-minded jurists who would overturn Warren and Burger Court era decisions and then follow a course of judicial restraint. The Senate of the mid- to late 1980s, which was a more ideologically liberal body than the Reagan administration, responded with an attempt to stem the conservative juridical tide with open ideological opposition. Writing only two years before the Bork nomination, Laurence Tribe argued that the nominee's "basic outlook and ideas about the law" were essential in the Senate's deliberation of a nominee.[15]

The emergence of ideology from a sublimated factor to a visible role allowed the nomination process to become a high-profile struggle between competing external camps. Before ideology was publicly acknowledged as a critical factor in public support, public campaigns would have been meaningless. But now groups on both sides can use public campaigns to bluntly portray the appointment as either harmful or helpful to the political goals of their members.

The intrusion of ideology also affected the criteria publicly acknowledged for an acceptable justice. In this new climate, liberals and conservatives have added more, but starkly different, criteria to their standard for a good justice. Liberals generally have sought a new justice who is sensitive to human rights and understands the plight of the powerless.[16] But conservatives generally have looked for a nominee who will interpret the U.S. Constitution strictly, preserve states' rights, and limit the power of the federal government.

Another ideology-related factor was the existing balance on the Court. Presidents justify selecting more ideologically extreme nominees not in order to stack the court with their ideological clones but to offer balance. For example, one Clinton administration vetter suggested that they were forced to consider ideology: "[The administration] faces a difficult challenge. Ideally, it should temper the role that ideology plays in the selection of Supreme Court justices, but at the same time it cannot be oblivious to the need to balance the court after a long series of conservative nominees."[17]

However, opposition forces also use the argument of balance by suggesting that the nominee should be rejected if he or she apparently departs sharply from the positions of the previous nominee. Obviously the argument is pressed when the nominee is viewed as further from the group's positions than the retiring justice and therefore more dangerous to the group's objectives. Antonin Scalia faced only mild opposition at least partly because the retiring justice, Chief Justice Warren Burger, was already perceived as a conservative. However, the Robert Bork nomination only one year later was seen as tilting the Court toward the right because Bork as a conservative was tapped to replace a justice who was viewed as more centrist, thus inciting opposition.

One example of this balance-tipping campaign is the battle over abortion. For abortion-related groups, the stakes in judicial nomination have become high. The *Roe v. Wade* decision in 1973 was a landmark decision by the Court to overturn a plethora of state abortion laws and move the abortion debate to the national political level. Pro-choice groups reveled not only in the direction of the decision but also in its scope.

But the *Roe* decision did not conclude the debate over abortion. Rather, it placed it high on the agenda of national politics, guaranteeing it would affect not only presidential and congressional elections but also Supreme Court appointments. Ever since the *Roe* decision, pro-life groups have labored to overturn or at least limit the breadth of the decision through constitutional amendments (albeit unsuccessfully) and the Supreme Court nomination process (more successfully). Following the election of two Republican presidents back to back in the 1980s and the appointment of a majority of the justices, group expectations were high by the early 1990s that the decision was doomed.

However, the *Planned Parenthood of Southeastern Pennsylvania v. Casey* decision did not provide the margin on the Court to overturn *Roe*, as had been widely predicted.[18] A trio of justices—ironically all Republican appointees of presidents dedicated to overturning *Roe*—carved out a centrist position on abortion that won the day in *Planned Parenthood of Southeastern Pennsylvania v. Casey*. The Court, led by Sandra Day O'Connor, Anthony Kennedy, and David Souter, upheld a constitutional right to abortion but enabled states to impose restrictions on that right as long as they did not constitute an undue burden on a woman's choice.[19]

But the dangers to *Roe* were still real in the minds of pro-choice advocates. For most pro-choice groups, the Court's position was highly unsatisfactory in that their goal was to return to the original provisions of the *Roe* decision. The efforts to achieve that result legislatively had been stymied by the Congress's failure to pass the Freedom of Choice Act, which would have denied states the right to restrict abortions before fetal viability.

Supreme Court vacancies under Democratic presidents were opportunities to turn the tide away from restrictions on *Roe*. For the National Abortion Rights Action League (NARAL), the National Organization for Women (NOW), and other pro-choice groups, the tide could be turned if replacements for existing justices supported *Roe* or at least opposed further erosion of the decision.

Similarly, pro-life groups viewed vacancies filled by Republican presidents as opportunities to tilt the Court toward a wholesale rejection of *Roe*. From the pro-life perspective, Justices Sandra Day O'Connor and David Souter had moved too far away from the position of overturning *Roe* to reverse themselves. Perhaps Justice Anthony Kennedy would join a new and solid anti-*Roe* majority on the Court, when one could be formed.

Both liberal and conservative groups view Supreme Court appointments as dangerous times when their gains can be taken from them. The Reagan-Bush appointments promised to undermine decisions favorable to liberal groups, and the Clinton appointments threatened to do the same for conservatives. The seesaw composition of the Court—a small number of individuals can tip the Court's balance on a host of policy issues—invites participation in the high-stakes game of Supreme Court nominations.

Both groups have acquired long memories over the past 30-plus years of confirmation battles and are eager to fight the last war over again. For example, following Clinton's election and the prospect of a Supreme Court nomination process, one conservative legal activist, warming to the possibility of a pitched battle, commented, "It'd be fun if it was Anita Hill."[20]

The Democratization of Political Selection

Still another force that would motivate external players is legitimating their role in this formerly exclusive process. The increasing democratization of political selection in American politics, from popular election of senators to direct primary elections for the selection of party nominees, has been a staple of American political history.

The framers' model was quite different. At the time of the writing of the Constitution, public involvement in politics was minimal. The election of the president was handled by elites, as was the Senate, which was selected by state legislators. The only democratically elected body was the House of Representatives. But even the electorate for that body was limited to white male property owners.

Over the next 200 years, American politics shifted in the direction of greater democracy in the selection of governing officials. The electoral process in presidential campaigns, once limited to an aristocratic exchange pursued by social and political elites through the media of correspondence and pamphlets, by the late 1820s became vulgarized with rallies, bonfires, and a mass-oriented press.[21] Although the electoral college still exists, the legal constraints in many states on who is certified as an elector (only those representing the party receiving the most votes) and how the elector votes (only for the party's nominee) have reduced its role to near-insignificance. The mass of voters in each state selects the president today. In addition, the suffrage has been expanded to include elements of the population previously excluded.

The selection of U.S. senators is now conducted through direct election. But even more, senators have become closer to their constituencies in other ways, thus undermining the distance the Constitution originally imposed. Senators go home more often, receive more mail, and campaign longer for reelection than they did in the past.

Although this democratization had already occurred for other political positions, the process of confirming justices until recently had been largely immune to such forces. However, over time, the president and the Senate's greater proximity to the electorate made inevitable the democratization of the confirmation process for the judiciary. Once the barrier was broken and external player involvement was considered legitimate and even healthy for the selection process, then external players—interest groups, the press, and even the public—felt no compunctions about participating in a formerly elite-defined process.

Governing in Public

Related to growing democratization of the selection process has been a mounting expectation of transparency in governmental action. Compared with just half a century ago, far more of what occurs in American national government today is deemed potentially open to public scrutiny.

This applies to the electoral process, where voters expect to know much more about candidates for office, especially the presidency, than they did in the past. With the required submission of financial records, press scrutiny of personal activities, and the assistance of their opponents, the voters become privy to a great deal more of a candidate's personal life. Candidates feel obligated to expose themselves to public view to pass the litmus test of character. The shrinking of the candidate's private life extends to the sphere of public office as well. Public disclosure rules mandate the release of private financial information about public officials.

Not only is individual information considered germane to the public interest but also the public policy process generally is subject to greater public scrutiny. Open meetings are expected in public life. With C-SPAN and CNN, more and more of the policy-making process is open to public view. Granted, most of the public policy process remains obscure to Americans and even to other elites because it hardly fits news values.[22]

But the potential for immediate and broad exposure now exists. Formerly anonymous agencies, events, and people can suddenly become highly newsworthy. The story of the machinations of a little-known Marine colonel named Oliver North in the Iran-contra affair is the classic example of a process not only going public but also quickly triggering saturation coverage in the press. Public scandals such as the House banking abuses, Iran-contra, and the Clinton impeachment process violently thrust administration officials, members of Congress, and others into the public eye.

But scandals are not the only reason for sudden exposure. Ongoing news stories with new angles, familiar persons, or conflict between powerful individuals contribute to the making of news.[23] In fact, a variety of factors intervene in the decision of what becomes newsworthy, factors that can be brought to bear in a situation to lift it from complete obscurity to wide public familiarity.

Increased public interest in national politics, which characterized the last half of the twentieth century, fed media status and led to greater investment in newsgathering and surveillance. The search for more and more news was the unintended by-product of the addition of all-news networks—CNN and C-SPAN—and the competition with the three major networks for news programming. The 1980s was the decade of news. News became a profitable entity of the three major networks, and, in turn, a greater proportion of the broadcast day was devoted to news. Moreover, independent news networks burst onto the scene and captured a faithful audience of news junkies.

The big break for Cable News Network (CNN) as the primary source of many Americans who were not news junkies was the Persian Gulf War in early 1991. Fox News experienced a similar boost from the war in Iraq. C-SPAN, which opened in 1978 with coverage of the House and then expanded with a second network covering the Senate, by the Bork hearings in 1987 had found its niche. One year after the hearings, an estimated 20 million Americans watched C-SPAN monthly.[24]

But news networks, particularly 24-hour ones, require quite a lot of news to fill the allotted time. CNN and C-SPAN fill that 24 hours with political news. Other programs, such as television talk shows, also have focused on political subjects and fed the demand for political news.

In turn, these news networks contributed to greater news emphasis by the traditional networks. The other television networks expanded news programming in part to compete with the all-news networks but in addition because news had become profitable.

Financial difficulties in the 1990s fostered a cutback in news organization budgets. However, the late 1990s produced a series of news stories to maintain public interest. The Monica Lewinsky scandal, the Clinton impeachment, the contested election of 2000, 9/11, and wars in Afghanistan and Iraq all contributed to public attention to national politics. Instead of shrinking news options, news networks proliferated with the addition of MSNBC and CNBC.

The rise in news also increased the public nature of standard government events. Television coverage of Congress, allowed first by the House in 1978, became a staple of C-SPAN and a regular feature in millions of homes with cable. The floor proceedings of the House and Senate received priority in the daily schedule of C-SPAN's two networks. Moreover, routine congressional committee proceedings earned a level of national attention unknown prior to the 1980s.[25]

Committee action also became more frequently shown on national television. By 1987, congressional committees were routinely aired on C-SPAN and CNN, occasionally with live coverage during major news stories, such as the Iran-contra hearings. Public airing of the hearings of the Iran-contra committee, the Senate Whitewater committee, and the impeachment of the president marked the 1980s and 1990s.

This development of extensive broadcasting of committee hearings was relatively recent. Before the 1970s, committee hearings were only rarely televised, due to individual committees' restrictions on their access. One of the best known exceptions was the Army-McCarthy hearings in 1954, which were televised live on ABC and the now defunct Dumont Network. But rule reforms of the early 1970s that opened hearings to broadcast coverage, as well as members' increasing comfort with television, facilitated almost universal television access to committee hearings and deliberations.

Some senators saw television coverage of committee hearings as an opportunity to gain public notice to further their agenda. Senator George Mitchell of Maine attracted national attention through his role in the Iran-contra hearings in 1987 and soon was elected Democratic Party leader in the Senate. Senator Al D'Amato of New York similarly sought to enhance his public image through his chairmanship of the Senate Whitewater Committee in the 1990s.

By 1987, the networks faced the dilemma of deciding which of the many available committee hearings to cover. With its jurisdiction over issues such as abortion, gun control, and the death penalty, the Judiciary Committee by the mid-1980s had become one of the more widely publicized committees.[26]

The move to open committee hearings obviously affected the Judiciary Committee's consideration of Supreme Court nominations. Hearings for Supreme Court nominations were televised live. New congressional rules on openness and the new presence of C-SPAN and CNN offered the vehicle for such coverage.

On June 14, 1993, CNN aired live President Clinton's mid-day announcement of Judge Ginsburg's nomination. More than 20 years earlier, President Nixon received similar network attention when announcing two appointments in 1971, but before C-SPAN and CNN, live television coverage of Supreme Court announcements was unusual. The preceding factors all have contributed to the emergence of the public process of judicial selection, even before the nomination of Robert Bork. The Bork nomination did not change the process. Rather, it became the landmark confirmation process because the conditions were in place by 1987 to make it so.

Creating a Vacuum

Traditional players, particularly the president, have created a vacuum for external players to carve out new roles for themselves. When the process is elongated and conducted in a highly public fashion, including a well-publicized interview and successions of trial balloons, groups and the press seize the opportunity to shape the direction of the process.

For example, President Bill Clinton's indecisiveness during a highly public process in 1993 and again in 1994 signaled to groups and the press that he could be influenced by their private and public efforts to shape the outcome. Following Governor Mario Cuomo's withdrawal, one Democratic strategist accurately predicted that "every interest group with a candidate will be lobbying hard."[27] Had the administration quickly moved to a candidate after Cuomo's decision, no vacuum would have existed. Interest group lobbying in the selection stage would have been nipped in the bud.

Trial balloons also create the opportunity for external force involvement. When administrations leak names on short lists, then groups and the press seize the opening to discuss the names as they would any other appointment. The Clinton administration did this repeatedly. Rather than announce an appointment, the White House released a list or even the name of a single individual under serious consideration. For example, in 1993, had the White House acted with dispatch to nominate Bruce Babbitt, it is highly unlikely environmental groups would have actively opposed his confirmation. (They opposed his nomination because they preferred having him stay at Interior where he could directly help him.) But the release of his name while he was still under consideration offered the opening for environmental groups to voice opposition.

Obviously, trial balloons place potential nominees in an awkward position. Essentially, they become sitting ducks for media scrutiny—their names hung out in the public arena. This process is particularly painful when administration officials seem to concentrate publicly on a single individual. This may be in response to journalistic focus on a single individual, but administration officials feed this tendency by focusing on certain individuals—one at a time. The result is a tortuous public rejection of a candidate, usually due to the appearance of external pressure.

Vacuums also occur when the White House conveys the message that the president is not committed to a particular goal. Clinton lacked such commitment, whereas both Nixon and Reagan saw filling Supreme Court vacancies as part of a larger ideological mandate. Both had used the Court's decisions as campaign themes. Supreme Court appointments were critical components of their commitment to the electorate to shape public policy and the governance process.

The president's own decision-making style affects the vacuum for external group involvement. Presidents Nixon, Reagan, and George H. W. Bush preferred secrecy and a narrow circle of advisors in decision making. Clinton, however, sought input from a broad array of sources. The administration included the legal community and groups in a way unfamiliar to recent appointments. The president frequently consulted with various senators from both parties and especially members of the Senate Judiciary Committee. But the Clinton consultations moved far beyond the confines of the U.S. Senate. In considering Bruce Babbitt, for example, Clinton even called Arizona's governor Fife Symington, a Republican, to inquire about Babbitt.[28]

Another component in opening up a vacuum is the speed of decision making. Some presidents, such as Ronald Reagan and George W. Bush, were known for quick decision making. Others, like Clinton and Carter, were less decisive. While serving as a presidential assistant, George Stephanopoulos confessed that Clinton "never makes a decision."[29] Clinton's manner of decision making was to collect as much information as possible before reaching closure. The president enjoyed long policy discussions with no real solution. He was open to input, welcomed it, and even desperately sought it again and again.

Moreover, Clinton was hesitant to delegate authority to a central figure, such as a powerful chief of staff. During both the Ginsburg and Breyer nomination processes, his chief of staff was his friend from kindergarten, Mack McLarty. However, McLarty's role essentially was that of another advisor to the president and not as a gatekeeper responsible for structuring the president's day to expedite decision making.

By the time of the Breyer nomination, White House Counsel Lloyd Cutler apparently was willing to play that role specifically in this area. He urged Clinton to come to closure quickly, thus helping the president avoid a repeat of the extensive press criticism of administration indecisiveness that had appeared the previous year. Clinton's decision-making process resulting in Breyer's appointment, although much longer than those of his two predecessors, lasted only six weeks as compared with the three months he used to make the decision to nominate Ginsburg.

Presidential indecisiveness mobilizes group and press involvement because effects by external players are still possible. Armed with faxed press releases and available spokespersons, groups are ready to offer the news media information on a continuing news story. Knowing the president is still deliberating, external players use inside and outside strategies to affect the outcome.

When a vacuum exists, external players use the opportunity to attempt to shape the process. Supporters of various candidates reach into the process and attempt to tilt it in their direction. External groups seemingly understand that the president's mind is hardly settled on any nominee. Hence, the groups can freely favor or oppose potential candidates and know that their efforts may very well lead the president for or against the object of their lobbying.

Effects on External Players

But how did these factors affect the behavior of each external player? Taking each external player individually, we can examine how these motives have shaped their perception of their role in the process and motivated their entrance into judicial appointment politics.

The Groups

The explanation for interest group involvement plainly revolves around protection of their perceived interests. Historically, groups have gathered to shape policy they believe affects the pursuit of their interests. Yet, lobbying had initially targeted only the legislative and executive branches.

Group interest in the Courts has emerged, as previously discussed, as groups have felt the effects of Court decisions on their policy objectives. They have seen the Court set policy in areas directly affecting their interests. The pro-life movement mobilized after the *Roe v. Wade* decision, and the pro-choice camp experienced a similar reinvigoration after the *Webster v. Reproductive Health Services* decision in 1989.[30] Affirmative action advocates and opponents have been subject to the shifting directions of the Court on the issue and repeatedly have sought to shape those positions.[31]

Groups have sought to use litigation to accomplish group goals. The litigation strategy has been the tool of last resort for most groups frustrated with the inaction or negative actions of political institutions. This method has been employed when legislative efforts largely have failed or promised only slow achievement of group objectives. Even groups originally not known as legal advocacy groups, such as environmental organizations, have sought to influence the Court's decisions.[32] Nevertheless, groups have used legal suits or amici curiae—friend of the Court briefs—to further policy objectives.[33]

Group litigious involvement has spiraled as groups respond to one another in the legal arena. One set of groups will turn to the courts to achieve decisions sympathetic to their policy goals, prompting an opposing group to seek legal redress to limit or overturn the first group's success.

Since it is the individuals on the Court who cast the votes and write the opinions, quite naturally groups have turned to influencing those who serve on the Court. Overt lobbying such as exists in the legislative or executive branches is frowned upon within the culture of the Court. However, groups have expanded their efforts to affect the initial selection of those who actually determine Court policy. During Republican administrations, conservatives have concluded they could shift the balance of the Court through successful eleva-tion of their own lower level judicial stars. Liberals, in turn, have mobilized to counter such efforts. The reverse is true in Democratic administrations.

Organizationally, groups benefit from controversial nomina-tions. The intensity of their role helps maintain the support of group members and supporters by fueling the perception of influence and, therefore, continued need for their existence. The Bork nomination, for example, was a windfall for those groups forming the anti-Bork coalition. They mobilized constituency interest in their groups, and then their efforts had spillover effects for the groups' organizational needs, such as membership, donations, and an overall reinforced com-mitment to the goals of the group.

These groups succeed in conveying the impression of being pow-erful entities in the nomination process. Hence, the perception is fostered that those involved in future nominations—whether at the White House or in the Senate—must consider the power of these groups to affect their plans.

However, their presence has hardly been benign. It has helped turn Supreme Court nominations into major battlegrounds for competing interest groups. Ideological, labor, educational, and women's groups have used mass media campaigns in recent nominations to sway pub-lic opinion and indirectly affect the outcome in the Senate.[34]

Interest groups' advertisements in print and broadcast media encourage the involvement of interested citizens. The battle over con-troversial nominees now is waged over the airwaves and in national magazines and newspapers. Anti-Bork forces reported they spent under $2 million on paid advertising, and a pro-Bork supporter suggested the anti-Bork forces spent $10 to 15 million to defeat his nomination.[35] As with electoral campaigns, the bulk of that amount probably was spent on media advertising. Even the lower figure of those two, although a pittance compared to major corporate advertising budgets, is astronomical when contrasted with the absence of any such spending on previous nominees.

The News Media

Given the groups' efforts to use the media to win confirmation battles, it is not surprising that another new player is the press. The news media find that Supreme Court nominations are big news stories, particularly when the White House, the Senate, and various groups collide. Bolstered by interest group leaders who salivate at the prospect of potential vacancies and warn of dire consequences if the other side prevails, news stories have touted the news value of judicial selection.[36]

Indeed, public interest in the confirmation process soars when the nominee is controversial. For example, the networks sensed that the Clarence Thomas–Anita Hill imbroglio was compelling news for the public. Combined, the three major television networks devoted 66 hours to the second round of Clarence Thomas hearings after Anita Hill's sexual harassment charges surfaced.[37] Public interest seemed to justify network decisions to preempt large blocks of previously scheduled entertainment programming. An estimated 30 million viewers watched the first night of the second round of Thomas hearings.[38] According to one survey, 86 percent of Americans said they had watched at least part of the television broadcast of Anita Hill's charges against Clarence Thomas.[39]

The press covers the process now *precisely* because it is so public. The battle by the White House, senators, and competing interest groups is waged before cameras and print journalists, and that very effort to go public attracts press interest. Moreover, the players in the process today are accustomed to speaking to the press in other settings, and doing so in a language the press understands.

Public interest groups particularly have a lengthy history of interacting with the press. They know how to frame the stakes of nominations in terms Americans clearly understand. Group leaders articulate to the press the stakes of these appointments, as they perceive them, for the constituents of the group or society at large. For example, women's groups discuss the effects of a certain nominee's appointment on the rights of women in areas such as abortion, sexual harassment, and comparable worth. Since these issues already have attracted press notice in other forums, they heighten the newsworthiness of the nomination process.

The objective of interest group communication with the press is not primarily the press itself, but the attentive public the press can reach. Within that broader public is a more important public—potential supporters. Groups use media messages to signal those who either belong to the group or, more likely, at least serve as a natural constituency for the group, such as African Americans for civil rights groups or fundamentalist Christians for the religious right. Signaling is designed primarily to shape public opinion and, for a minority of those supporters, mobilize them to contact senators, write letters to the editor, or offer donations to the group.

Supreme Court nomination stories indisputably are newsworthy today. All the elements of news are present—conflict, drama, uniqueness, the presence of well-known personalities.[40] Because the news value is apparent, the Supreme Court selection process has become a certified media event. News organizations devote resources to their coverage of the process. Some news organizations now undertake far-reaching campaigns to investigate nominees, either through direct investigative reporting or indirectly through reliance on interest group efforts.

Given this expanded interest group involvement and reliance on the press for external strategy implementation, as well as enhanced press resources to cover the process, it should not be surprising that news coverage of nominations has indeed increased. Table 3.1 shows the coverage of the Supreme Court nomination process from Sandra

Table 3.1
Changes in Number of *New York Times* and *Time* Magazine
Stories of Supreme Court Nominations before and after Bork
Nomination Process

	NYT	Time
Pre-Bork		
Stewart/O'Connor	36	4
Burger/Rehnquist	54	4
Scalia	12	2
Post-Bork		
Powell/D. Ginsburg/Kennedy	63	15
Brennan/Souter	53	15
Marshall/Thomas	35	16
White/Ginsburg	42	7
Increase Post-Bork over Pre-Bork	38%	300%

Day O'Connor in 1981 to Ruth Bader Ginsburg in 1993 in the *New York Times* and *Time* magazine. The stories represent the period from the retirement of the sitting justice through the confirmation of a successor. The greater coverage of the Ruth Bader Ginsburg nomination process versus that of Clarence Thomas is a function of the length of the selection stage in the Ginsburg case (nearly three months) and the short, although highly intense, period of the second stage of the Thomas confirmation hearings involving Anita Hill's accusations.

This table accentuates the change that occurred in news coverage of Supreme Court nominations post–Robert Bork. The Bork nomination clearly marked a change in the newsworthiness of Supreme Court nominations. The number of news stories in the *New York Times* increased by 38 percent between the pre-Bork and post-Bork periods. *Time* magazine coverage was even more dramatic.

The table also reveals that press interest did not wane following the Souter or Thomas nominations, although not all nominations will receive that intensity of coverage. Interest may flag if a succession of noncontroversial nominees occurs. But, given presidential propensity

Table 3.2
Placement in Network News Broadcast of Stories of Supreme Court
Nominees 1990–1994 (ABC, NBC, and CBS combined)

Placement	Souter (%)	Thomas (%)	Ginsburg (%)	Breyer (%)
1st third	54	53	70	66
2nd	34	36	23	31
3rd	12	11	7	3
Total	100	100	100	100
	(N = 38)	(N = 105)	(N = 44)	(N = 34)

Source: Vanderbilt University Television News Abstracts Archive.

to seek to pack the Court, the reality of divided government, and other motives for opposition stated earlier, that is unlikely.

Another way to measure newsworthiness is the salience of news stories of a Supreme Court nomination by media organizations. Does a nomination story receive priority over other news? A study of all stories of nominations broadcast on network evening news between 1990 and 1994 was conducted to test whether this thesis is true. The study examined the placement of news stories of four nominations (Souter, Thomas, Ginsburg, Breyer) on the three major network television evening news broadcasts. Table 3.2 divides evening news broadcasts into thirds (10-minute segments) and categorizes nomination news stories according to their placement in those groupings.

This table demonstrates that nomination stories have been highly newsworthy. At least half of the stories about each nomination were aired in the first third of broadcasts. The salience of these stories may be related to their infrequency. With only nine justices serving life terms, personnel change on the Court is relatively rare compared with other types of news.

Stories about the initial announcement of a Supreme Court nomination merited high placement. That was especially true in the case of Stephen Breyer, whose announcement was divided over two days— the Friday on which the announcement was made and the following Monday, when a formal ceremony occurred. Broadcast news coverage on Monday also showed the White House's staged photo opportunity of the president jogging with Judge Breyer.

But such attention also can be attributed to some controversy associated with nominations. The Thomas confirmation hearings, for example, attracted high priority on evening news broadcasts, especially during the second round involving Anita Hill's accusations.

And still another factor is the routine of press coverage. The first day of confirmation hearings of even the less controversial nominations—Souter, Ginsburg, and Breyer—also received broadcast news attention because of the drama of the setting. However, that coverage did not extend to subsequent days because of the lack of controversy.

The involvement of groups and the media has altered the communication methods of the formal players in the process. In a process gone public, the old systems of communication and persuasion are no longer adequate. Backroom negotiation has been at least partly supplanted. Even when it occurs, it does so under the shadow of potential immediate public disclosure by one or more of the participants. The motive to disclose private negotiations is strong in that the first to speak to the press may shape the media's and the public's perceptions.

Under the old system, interest group lobbyists, White House staff, Senate staff, and the legal community could communicate directly and privately. Interaction was personal because it involved a small circle of participants.

The players today include a larger array of physically distant groups and individuals unable to sit down together or pass each other in hallways. As stated earlier, more than 300 interest group organizations were involved in the anti-Bork coalition.[41]

The new means of communication utilized today are mass media outlets. Only through mass media can groups reach the masses of supporters they want to become engaged in the nomination process. Moreover, the newly legitimized player—the public—relies exclusively on the media to glean information about the process. Hence, television, radio, newspapers, news magazines, and the Internet play far greater roles in the communication of news about the nomination process to active players than ever before.

The involvement of the press introduces a new element to the process. As with other processes in which the mass public is expected to play a role, such as presidential selection, Supreme Court nominations have become oriented toward media presentation. The White House, the Senate, interest groups, and even the nominee move through the confirmation stage sensitive to image making and the media's role. Each player attempts to employ the media to shape the image of the process and the nominee.

The manipulation of media images suggests that the news media act merely as a vehicle for others' ambitions. However, the news media also act as an independent influence in the process. They not only transmit the views of other actors but also filter those views by using organizational and professional imperatives. These imperatives shape newsgathering and reporting.[42]

The classic news story was the Clarence Thomas confirmation, with its combination of recurring news interests—sexual scandal, race, and ideological conflict—and the clash of competing interest groups signaling to the press the issues involved in the process. Because of the media imperatives of reporting news, after the announcement of Anita Hill's charges, the Thomas nomination garnered saturation coverage. According to an NBC News executive vice president, the networks latched onto the Thomas story because of its combination of recurring news interests—sex, race, and politics: "Very rarely had we seen anything like this where all of these issues converged in one place at one time."[43]

Media imperatives determine the extent of news coverage devoted to a topic and the angle offered. A nomination process has the potential for high impact on a large number of Americans, but absent other values, such as conflict or drama, there will be minimal news coverage.

The potential effect of media imperatives is a difference in the conduct and the outcome of the process. But such effect has yet to be conclusively demonstrated. However, this perception that such an effect exists is demonstrated in the following conclusion, drawn by a Bork supporter after Bork's defeat, that the press coverage contributed to a misunderstanding of the nominee: "Viewers rarely got to see answers of any length or complexity. Sentences were selected for presentation according to what a program's producers judged to be the essence of Bork's philosophy or the day's important trend."[44]

News imperatives guarantee that newsworthy angles of a story receive prominence in the news portrayal. For television, especially, the personalization of the news enhances its visual attractiveness and sustains audience interest. Hence, focusing on the human interest aspects of a nominee meets media imperatives.

Plainly, a media-oriented process reshapes the judicial selection process. It affects the type of communication carried on by principal players in the process. In the traditional process, legal community pressure and White House lobbying were internal, private processes. Communication was interpersonal, and persuasion was personalized.

Now, interpersonal communication is supplemented by mediated communication. Instead, players in the process use media to acquire public support and communicate with other players, subject to the filter of the imperatives of the media.

The presence of the media can become so apparent that it becomes the story. In the case of the Thomas confirmation, the news media themselves became news when two journalists broke the Anita Hill story. They became embroiled in the confirmation process as some media critics and Clarence Thomas supporters lashed out at them for reporting the results of a confidential investigation. One of the journalists, Nina Totenberg, publicly defended her role and participated in an on-air verbal clash with Senator Alan Simpson of Wyoming. After the confirmation vote, both Totenberg and *Newsday* reporter Timothy Phelps resisted a Senate special prosecutor's efforts to discover the source of their reports.[45]

The Public

The involvement of other external forces—groups and the news media—stimulates public involvement. As press coverage increases, the public nature of the process spirals. It appears that as the event acquires a higher profile in public debate, the involvement of the mass public increases. In recent nominations (such as Bork and Thomas), it has reached the point of saturation coverage, where the attentive public begins to form judgments and join the debate. Polling organizations survey the public on aspects of Supreme Court nominations, particularly on whether a nominee should be confirmed. Conducting such polls and disseminating their results in a sense legitimates the public's role. Why ask the public unless public opinion matters in the judicial selection process?

Groups frame the issues in Supreme Court nominations in a context encouraging a public role. For example, groups opposing Robert Bork argued that his views as a Supreme Court justice (based on his views as a scholar or judge) would take the country backward in terms of social progress on issues such as race relations, gender equity, and abortion rights. Both sides of the abortion issue have framed Supreme Court nominations as relevant to their cause. In addition, groups mobilize members to become engaged in political debate over nominations by lobbying senators about their potential confirmation vote.

The combination of news coverage, group appeals (which stimulates more news coverage), and polling facilitates public opinion as a factor in judicial selection. The public is legitimated as a player by other external forces that seek to shape and use public opinion to support their efforts.

In summary, the changes in the nomination process can be attributed to the need of both internal and external players for an extension of the conflict beyond its historically narrow confines. The scene was set for a new, more public process to emerge that would involve other actors—interest groups, the news media, and public opinion.

4

New Roles for External Players

The Supreme Court nomination process today is not one where those involved are merely the traditional, Constitutionally defined players. External forces play significant new roles. Interest groups, the press, and the public now perform functions within the process that are affected by and affect each other's involvement, as well as the roles of the traditional players—the president, the Senate, and the Court. This chapter enumerates permanent roles now performed by players who only occasionally participated in the past.

New Roles for Groups

The images of interest group representatives sitting in a row at a witness table in front of Senate Judiciary Committee members and a bank of photographers are now staples in the Senate confirmation process. More than that, groups now issue press releases and hold news conferences to affect the president's selection of a nominee and even air television and print advertisements, write op-ed columns, and conduct a host of other activities designed to affect the Senate vote on a Supreme Court nominee.

The role of groups has become legitimate in the eyes of other players. As mentioned earlier, Senate consideration of the views of various groups in Supreme Court nominations is not new. Barbara Perry has concluded that religion, race, and gender were significant in nearly a dozen appointments to the Court over its more than 200-year history, and that such consideration was linked to electoral support by various groups.[1] The creation of Catholic, Jewish, and women's seats occurred during the past century because of pressure from various groups.

Group pressure has not been limited to demographic representation. In fact, it centers primarily on policy agreement, including both overriding ideological correlation, such as a conservative nominee satisfying conservative groups, and specific issue agreement on single issues important to particular vocal groups, such as abortion or civil rights groups.

Groups have adopted specific roles in the process that help shape its conduct and potential outcome. Those roles begin not with the announcement of a nominee but even earlier in the selection stage. Groups increasingly have viewed the selection stage as critical in securing a nominee who reflects group interests. This is particularly true for groups supportive of the administration, whose views carry weight with a sympathetic president. Interest groups perform essentially six roles in the nomination process: establishing nominee standards, nominating candidates to the president, screening candidates on the short list, researching the nominee, determining Senate questions, and making the public case on the nominee.

Establishing Nominee Standards for Presidential Selection

Today, groups increasingly affect the yardstick presidents use to sort through potential nominees. During the 2004 general election, for example, candidate John Kerry accepted the litmus test sought by pro-choice groups when he asserted that he would choose only those nominees who supported *Roe v. Wade*.

Another recent criterion set by interest groups is gender. Women's groups lobbied for a female justice before Sandra Day O'Connor's appointment in 1981. President Reagan accepted their criteria when, as a presidential candidate, he announced that his first appointment to the court would be a woman.[2]

This criterion became important again in 1993, when President Clinton sought a replacement for Byron White. Women's groups asserted that the appointment should be used to select another woman for the court to reinforce the message that women should not be merely tokens. They also expressed some disappointment in Justice Sandra Day O'Connor, who did not mirror their views, particularly on abortion.

In 1993, leaders of women's groups conducted both internal and external campaigns to establish that criterion for presidential selection. In fact, the gender criterion became so important to women's groups during 1993 that at the end of the nomination stage, although some of them initially had been dissatisfied with Ruth Bader Ginsburg, they began to offer unqualified support in the face of the possible appointment of another male.

Opposition groups also help establish the criteria for selection. Publicly, they urge the administration to back away from litmus tests adopted by supportive groups. For example, conservatives sought to push the Clinton administration and its constituent interest groups apart. One conservative activist opined that Clinton's New Democrat image would be a farce if "Mr. Clinton allows the left wing of his party, and their interest group allies, to exact activist judicial payment for campaign support."[3]

They also pursue internal strategies, reinforcing their public message. Opposition groups privately warn the administration away from nominees they consider fair game for opposition, thus helping establish criteria for selection. In 1987, following the confirmation defeat of Robert Bork, liberal groups warned President Reagan that selecting another nominee like Robert Bork would lead to still another confirmation defeat.

Supportive groups can go both inside and outside to establish criteria for selection. Opposition groups typically are limited to using the press as the medium for communication with the administration. However, opposition party senators can convey a private message to the president of the group's perception of potential confirmation trouble for a specific nominee.

The role of groups in establishing criteria is hardly neutral in terms of effects on the selection process. Their involvement has resulted in a presidential selection process dominated by their expectations. Groups demand that their interests take priority in the selection process to assure that potential nominees reflect group positions. For example, in 1991 conservative groups were frustrated when Justice David Souter, once on the Court, proved to be as unreliable as social conservatives had feared during his confirmation process. They longed for an unmistakable conservative they could rally around and count on to overturn liberal opinions, particularly *Roe v. Wade*. They lobbied President George H. W. Bush to support an unambiguous conservative such as Clarence Thomas to secure their support during his upcoming reelection bid.[4] Similarly, in 1993 pro-choice groups took for granted that President Clinton would nominate a pro-choice advocate for the bench.

Groups drive presidents toward constituency choices to further group policy goals. In turn, presidents respond, because of their dependence on these groups to achieve their own goals. Presidents who pursue a consensual rather than a constituency approach to justice picking run the risk of alienating key group support, not only for the confirmation process but also for other presidential policy initiatives in the future, or even for reelection. Clearly, presidents do not always subscribe to group interests, but failure to do so could harm a president in a number of ways.

Yet, in certain situations constituency choices clearly are not in the best interest of presidents. When the opposition party controls the Senate, constituency choices have diminished prospects for victory. Or the president may not wish to endure a protracted conflict over a nominee, particularly when the president has other agenda interests and does not wish to expend valuable political capital.

However, the decision to opt for a consensual nominee, caused by a president's need to get an individual confirmed, can be taken as betrayal by groups. They need to be appeased to support consensual nominees. For example, Anthony Kennedy's nomination did not excite conservative groups. However, with his earlier unsuccessful nominations of constituency choices—Robert Bork and Douglas Ginsburg—Reagan had demonstrated his willingness to pursue the constituency route and satisfy conservative groups. Similarly, David Souter's nomination engendered only lukewarm support from conservative groups, who knew little about the New Hampshire judge. Bush Chief of Staff John Sununu sought to reassure them that Souter was one of them.

Nominating Candidates to the President

Groups play a critical role in suggesting a short list of candidates for presidential consideration. They are actively involved in feeding the administration lists of possible nominees. In addition, those candidates initiated by the administration typically are vetted through various groups. That vetting is abetted by the fact that many of those who sit in White House or Justice Department political appointee posts have been recruited from interest groups traditionally allied with the party: For the Democrats, examples include women's groups, pro-choice groups, labor, and racial and ethnic groups, and for the Republicans, business groups, the pro-life movement, and the religious right.

Group representatives serve in administration positions where they hold responsibility for vetting judicial nominees. For example, in the Clinton administration, Ricki Seidman served as deputy communications director in the White House, while Melanne Verveer held the post of deputy chief of staff in the Office of the First Lady. Both were former staffers at People for the American Way.

During the George W. Bush administration, social conservative groups offered names of conservative judges for presidential consideration, such as Justice Thomas for a possible chief justice vacancy.[5] Similarly, during the Clinton administration, women's groups contributed names of potential female nominees, including federal appellate judges Patricia Wald, Judith Kaye, and Amalya Kearse. For a time during one selection process, Clinton administration vetters were publicizing the names of several female state supreme court jurists whose names had been recommended by women's groups.

Screening Candidates on the President's Short List

Presidents usually begin the selection process with a relatively large number of potential nominees. For example, in 1993 Bill Clinton started with 42, although he later admitted only seven were seriously in play. The selection process is culling names down to a single one.

Groups understand this process and seek to participate in that culling. One way they do so is by raising potential problems they have identified through group research on prospective nominees. In the case of the Ginsburg nomination, for example, women's groups volunteered to the Clinton administration the information that Ginsburg had delivered a lecture at New York University criticizing the breadth of *Roe v. Wade* and that her opinions on the D.C. Circuit Court of Appeals had been more moderate than they had expected. One year later, the same groups informed the administration they would oppose Judge Richard Arnold because the Arkansas judge had made two decisions in favor of the exclusion of women from private clubs and parental notification on abortion.[6]

Even opposition groups can participate in the culling process, at least through the vehicle of press coverage. Opposition groups are able to gain some press notice during the process due to their predictability in providing the news value of conflict essential to news stories. Tom Jipping, director of the Judicial Monitoring Project, explained why his group received the attention it did: "The press thrives on conflict, and so the people that create the conflict are ones that get a lot of attention. Supporting [George H. W.] Bush's nominees doesn't create conflict. Opposing Clinton's does."[7]

Researching the Nominee

Although the expectation for Senate investigation of a nominee has increased dramatically in recent years, the staff required has not risen concomitantly. Hence, senators do not have the staff at their disposal to conduct full investigations, especially when other responsibilities still remain. One reporter reluctantly concluded: "All too often, it is the press or some private organization that does the kind of investigation that the Committee should do."[8] The Senate has come to rely on the investigative work of interest groups and the press to discover background information about a nominee. Interest groups, then, have acquired this research role to supplement staff work and to influence the Senate's inquiry. Obviously, such research is hardly neutral. It is designed to further the groups' claims about the nominee and affect individual senators' voting behavior.[9]

Determining Senate Questions

Interest groups also provide senators with written questions and expect them to be posed to nominees. Nominee questions often reflect the groups' interests more than the senators'. This practice was dramatically illustrated in 1993, when Senator Larry Pressler of South Dakota asked Judge Ginsburg how she felt about "arbitrary caps on damages." She replied: "Senator, I think you loaded that question by calling them arbitrary." Sheepishly, Pressler responded that the question was "one that one of my lawyers or someone sent in."[10]

Making the Public Case on the Nominee

Interest groups also apply to testify at confirmation hearings either for or against the nominee. The Bork nomination was the first when a lengthy list of groups sought to participate in hearings, especially to voice opposition to confirmation. Group testimony elongated the Bork hearings by stretching over several days.

But even when confirmation is certain, opposition groups still appear to make their public case against the nominee. In both the Ginsburg and Breyer nominations, pro-life groups testified against their respective confirmations. Ginsburg attracted opposition testimony from the Eagle Forum and the Conservative Coalition, despite the fact that Republican leaders such as Senate Majority Leader Bob Dole and Senator Orrin Hatch, ranking member on the Judiciary Committee, already had expressed support for her.[11]

New Roles for the Press

Similarly, the press has acquired new roles in the judicial selection process. These roles are not independent of other actors but form interplay among presidents, nominees, senators, groups, the public, and the press—with the press as the direct object of attention and each other player the target of press attention.

Publicly Scrutinizing Nominees

To a degree unknown before, the press has acquired the responsibility for scrutinizing the backgrounds of candidates for public office. This responsibility primarily has been directed at presidential candidates. However, as the Supreme Court nomination process has become a battleground between competing interest groups, the press has taken special notice of the nominees as objects of public interest. Groups feed this interest with reports on nominees designed to affect the image of the candidate in the public mind.

Moreover, stories about nominees become even more newsworthy when they correspond to other news stories. Sandra Day O'Connor was appointed at a time of intense public debate over the legal status of women, as evidenced by gender discrimination cases and the Equal Rights Amendment. A decade late, the accusations of sexual harassment against Clarence Thomas were raised in an atmosphere of public concern about sexual harassment in the workplace.

Some journalists conduct investigative work, but many rely on the research efforts of others, particularly groups. Opposition groups are more than happy to offer journalists information that might call into question the nominee's fitness. Another source for press scrutiny is the nominee questionnaire administered and issued by the Senate Judiciary Committee. In addition to personal financial information and background facts, the questionnaire requests a copy of every speech the nominee has given, every position held with various organizations, and the policy statements of those organizations with whom the nominee has affiliated. When the results are distributed to the press, the nominee's responses initiate news stories about financial net worth, membership in social clubs, and other potentially newsworthy information.

The questionnaire also can become fodder for senators' questions at committee hearings, thus provoking another round of publicity as reporters have the news peg of a senator posing a question. For example, in 1993 Senator Hatch used Ruth Bader Ginsburg's answer to a questionnaire query about the race and gender of her employees to note that she had never hired an African American as a clerk.[12]

Press scrutiny can be a significant factor in the outcome of a nomination. One example was the "nanny problem" in the early 1990s. In 1993, two of President Clinton's nominees for attorney general bowed out because they had hired illegal aliens as domestic help and, in one case, failed to pay Social Security taxes.[13] Judge Breyer and his wife similarly had failed to pay Social Security taxes for a part-time cleaning woman who was already receiving Social Security benefits. The problem was similar to that of the other Clinton nominees, but, unlike the other two, Breyer rectified the problem before it became public. However, in the wake of the previous news stories and the resulting clamor, Breyer's problem became news and scuttled his nomination prospects that year.

Prepping the Public for an Upcoming Vacancy and Nomination Process

The press also takes a role in preparing the public for a future vacancy and pending nomination process. Even before a retirement is announced, pundits speculate about who will leave the Court, when, and who the potential replacements will be. The prognostication is strongest with the juncture of a senior justice and the inauguration of a president who reflects the justice's ideology.[14]

Some of the most intense preannouncement speculation occurred during the George W. Bush presidency. With the last vacancy in 1994, Bush's inauguration in 2001 sparked a frenzy of guessing about pending retirements. The combination of a bench dominated by Republicans, some in their seventies, and the Oval Office occupied by a Republican fed rumors that two or perhaps three eventual retirements would occur during the first years of Bush's term. Speculation focused on Court members appointed by Republican presidents, such as Chief Justice William Rehnquist and associate justices Sandra Day O'Connor and John Paul Stevens, who were said to be on the verge of retirement. However, such conjecture remained only that, because none of the justices retired at that time.

Publicizing the Shifting Short List

Another new press role is publicizing the coming and going of potential nominees. Unlike most nominations in the past, the withdrawal of prominent candidates today has become a public exercise. For example, in 1993 the White House leaked the news that New York Governor Mario Cuomo was at the top of the administration's short list. Cuomo publicly toyed with the idea of the appointment, as if it were his for the asking, and then suddenly withdrew his name from consideration. The next year, Senate Majority Leader George Mitchell also withdrew his name from consideration after he was named as the likely nominee.

On the heels of apparent administration concentration on certain individuals, public withdrawals by likely nominees become significant events and, not surprisingly, the object of substantial news media coverage. Prominent withdrawals harm the White House's ability to frame the image of the process. The coverage may convey the impression the administration is having difficulty in choosing a candidate.

Establishing the Public Interview Process

Another point of press involvement is the public interview process. In various facets of personnel selection—nonprofit organizations, educational institutions, governmental bodies—public candidate interviews are now expected. Presidential candidates now often conduct high-profile public interviews to select vice presidential running mates.

Supreme Court nominations have taken on some of that appearance. Obviously, there is still not a formalization of the process: Presidential style still ranges from no public interviews to highly public sessions with prospective candidates for nomination. President Reagan adopted the former approach with Sandra Day O'Connor, who was quietly interviewed at the White House without press fanfare.[15] Similarly, in 1970 Richard Nixon met with potential nominee Harry Blackmun without any mention to the press.[16]

During a later selection stage, the White House announced that President George H. W. Bush had extended White House invitations to two candidates simultaneously, thus reducing the sense of inevitability of the appointment of a particular individual.

In 1993, President Bill Clinton did conduct a highly publicized interview that was thoroughly covered by the press. However, the process was applied to only a single candidate, Judge Stephen Breyer. The fact that Breyer was touted as the front-runner by some administration officials and that he was called out from his hospital bed to visit with the president, suggesting a great sense of urgency, heightened the significance of Breyer's interview. When Breyer faced intense scrutiny but was not selected in 1993, the Clinton administration learned a lesson and avoided any interviews the next time.

Presidents might not wish to conduct a public interview process. However, such a process serves White House purposes. A public interview process suggests the president is making progress on selection. It satisfies and channels the press's interest in the process.

On the other hand, public interviews heighten press scrutiny of particular candidates. In essence, the press is invited to examine all facets of the candidate or candidates, as well as to comment editorially on the fitness of the individual. In addition, press coverage encourages an interest group role in that reporters rely on sources and various groups typically are eager to weigh in on potential nominees, thus feeding more stories.

Helping Create a Short List

Still another event for press coverage is the periodic floating of various names by the administration for trial balloon purposes and the instantaneous reaction of senators and various groups. Trial balloons help the administration gauge potential group, press, and even public reaction to a prospective nominee before the administration commits to naming that individual.

Some names released to the press will not appear on the president's short list, despite the implication in the press leak. Those names are released for other purposes, such as recognition of the individual's career or communication to a particular group or set of groups that their preferred candidates have been included in the process, although perhaps not seriously. Richard Nixon even floated the name of Senator Robert Byrd of West Virginia, even though he had no intention of nominating the conservative Democrat who was a former member of the Ku Klux Klan. Rather, Nixon wanted senators to be relieved when he did not nominate Byrd and be more inclined to support another person just as conservative but not a former member of the KKK.[17]

Through news coverage, the press also plays its own role in creating the short list, particularly in conjunction with groups. News created by groups becomes the content of news stories. For example, groups may leak news about their preferred candidates to send signals to the administration, or they may attempt to make news by shooting down trial balloons sent up by the administration. For example, environmental groups opposed the potential nomination of Interior Secretary Bruce Babbitt in 1993 because they wanted him to stay at Interior. Their opposition became a major news story and provided the groups with the unusual opportunity to gain attention for their views about who should be a Supreme Court nominee.

Individual senators also use the forum of the press to affect the short list. For example, again in 1993, Senator Hatch used his appearances on television talk shows to signal his opposition to Babbitt because of his fears that Babbitt would be an effective political leader on the Court.

But the press also plays a role independent of interest group influence. Early in the Clinton presidency, for example, an article in *New Republic* listed prospective nominees and placed Ginsburg at the top of the list. Anthony Lewis assisted in keeping Ginsburg's name on the short list by chastising the women's groups attempting to take it off because of her views on the *Roe* decision.

In another instance, the *Washington Times* covered Bruce Babbitt in a series of investigative stories linking him with Las Vegas gambling debts.[18] The stories implied that Babbitt was less than Supreme Court material. The administration denied that the stories affected Clinton's decision making. Press Secretary Dee Dee Myers called them "old, rehashed. I think they've been discredited previously."[19] Yet, Babbitt was passed over by Clinton, twice.

Helping Create and Then Covering Media-Oriented Events

Supreme Court nominations have become open conflicts among elites in American politics. The ideological battle is arrayed with various players carrying the colors of differing ideologies. What a great story!

Since Robert Bork and Clarence Thomas, Supreme Court nominations have had the potential to become "hot" news stories. Journalists are somewhat frustrated when the battle is not joined. *Newsweek's* CW (conventional wisdom) column admitted that the Ginsburg nomination in the wake of the Clarence Thomas hearings was a disappointment. "The Supreme Court isn't as much fun as it used to be. The CW congratulates the president on his perfect choice, but was secretly hoping for a controversial showboat."[20] A "controversial showboat" is attractive because it sells papers and boosts ratings. Conflict, drama, and unexpected behavior all aid that process.

News organizations, then, have their own agenda. News of controversial nominations excites interest by the more attentive audience. Scandal news, such as the allegations against Clarence Thomas, involves even the less attentive audience. Because conflict is such a paramount news value, it is difficult for some journalists to be satisfied with consensus appointments in that an opportunity is missed to cover an exciting news story.

Conflict is potentially high in certain media events, particularly confirmation hearings on a controversial nomination. Print reporters crowd press tables, and photographers gather in front for dramatic pictures, while television cameras are trained on the nominee and the senators to cover the battle royal.

Not surprisingly, then, the press has helped create the battlefields where ideological war can be waged. The major media event is the nominee's appearance before the Judiciary Committee. At no other time is the intersection of external and internal players so apparent. Senators, the nominee, interest groups, the White House, and even the press all are represented at these sessions. The nominee sits at a witness table facing the curved bench behind which committee members sit. But behind the nominee can be found the nominee's White House handlers, representatives from various interest groups waiting to testify or merely interested in noting the nominee's views on positions of interest to them, and, of course, the members of the press, taking notes and preparing the news copy that other players, including the public, will read or hear that evening or the next morning.

The hearings cater heavily to the news media, particularly the broadcast media. Senators know television cameras are there. C-SPAN airs the hearings live. CNN often does so, particularly on the first day. The major broadcast networks carry clips of the hearings on the first day, as well as on subsequent days if major news appears. Occasionally, such as in the case of the Thomas hearings after Anita Hill's accusations, the broadcast networks preempt other program to cover the hearings.

For the most part, the networks' reporters and cameras disappear after the first day in an noncontroversial hearing. There is no expectation of dramatic news unless some senator or group of senators is known to be in opposition and apt to use their allotted time to contend with the nominee.

Senators, the nominee, groups, and even the president, indirectly, are on stage during the several-day event that now constitutes Senate

Judiciary Committee hearings. Although other players, particularly many senators and groups, already have experienced this process, the nominee is a newcomer to it. In preparation for Senate hearings, the White House conducts "murder boards," mock sessions of committee hearings designed to prepare nominees for the scrutiny of hours of live televised Senate questioning. The magnitude of White House intervention in this process is one indication of the influence of television on the process and the extent to which an administration envisions confirmation hearings as an integral part of its larger image-making strategy.

With live televised coverage of the proceedings, poor performance by a nominee before the Judiciary Committee becomes the subject of national debate. It reflects negatively not only on the nominee but also on the president who is the nominee's sponsor. Nominee preparation becomes critical because a nominee's opposition forces use the platform of a national audience to undermine support from the public and within the Senate. Groups' own testimony follows that of the nominee and is designed to sway Senate committee votes and also to shape press and public attitudes toward the nominee because the press, interested in the conflict elements of the story, invariably covers opposition comments.

The nominee, then, is entering a broader fray in which he or she is another pawn in the struggle between long-standing competing positions on public policy, as well as on the role of the judicial branch. Lacking experience in such sessions, the nominee is ideally prepared through the murder boards run by the White House to operate within a potentially hostile environment or even a friendly one, to avoid the risk of making it hostile.

Assuming hostility from a committee dominated by the opposition party, the Reagan administration used a murder board to prepare Judge Bork for his grueling session before the committee. The practice has become standard for the subsequent nominees. For example, in 1993, Ruth Bader Ginsburg was subjected to a two-stage process. She was allowed to select briefers who would prepare her on specific aspects of the law. She spent one week with various legal scholars in areas such as religion, free speech, free press, and criminal law. One of her former law clerks took notes and prepared a summary of the sessions. The presenters briefed her on what was new in that particular area in order to, as she put it, "help me to bring it to the front of my mind."[21]

Then the White House trained her on presentation. They put her through three days of mock hearings where she endured question after question in lengthy sessions. Initially she was reluctant, but eventually she appreciated the experience: "I don't think that I would have, just on the basis of sheer endurance, managed the hearings as well, if I had not had three days of exposure to . . . 'we're going to keep on asking you these questions and you're going to keep on answering, even though you would like to call it off.'"[22]

Senators are well aware of the presence of cameras. Even when confirmation is a foregone conclusion, senators rarely dispense with their opportunity to speak at length before the cameras. Senator Howard Metzenbaum attempted to publicly chide Judge Breyer and commit him to Metzenbaum's views. At one point, Metzenbaum was even explicit about this goal:

> SENATOR METZENBAUM: All I am hoping to do in these hearings is maybe sensitize you enough, and when you get on the Supreme Court, maybe you will remember, gee, I remember those questions I had when I was appearing before the Judiciary Committee, maybe the milk of human kindness will run through you and you will not be so technical.
>
> JUDGE BREYER: I guarantee you, I will remember.[23]

Because all of the Senate Judiciary Committee members are expected to grill the nominee but have little to say, some senators use their moment before the cameras to make points unrelated to the nominee. Again, during the Breyer confirmation hearings, Republican Senator Strom Thurmond noted Breyer's Oxford years and his service in the army and then asked rhetorically if Breyer thought an Oxford education was incompatible with military service. Aware of the question's relevance to the president who nominated him, Breyer almost whispered, "No."[24]

As mentioned earlier, groups have joined the media event of televised confirmation hearings. Groups use hearings to signal not only the Senate but also their membership, the press, and the public about their reaction to the nominee. Ralph Nader testified against Breyer to claim he was too supportive of big business interests.[25] But such testimony becomes important primarily when there is no presumption of confirmation. Otherwise, it mainly satisfies group imperatives.

At confirmation hearings, White House and Justice Department minders sit behind the nominee to signal White House presence in the confirmation process and offer moral support to the nominee. Additionally, during breaks in the hearings, they mingle with the press to spin the testimony, when necessary, toward more positive coverage of the nominee.

Votes by the Judiciary Committee and the full Senate constitute two final points for news coverage. Negative votes or votes with uncertain outcomes obviously receive much more attention than favorable ones. But favorable ones still constitute at least some news value when any negative votes are cast.

The judicial selection process, for news purposes, constitutes a series of events, many of which have been transformed for the benefit of the press. With various access points to the process, it is no wonder the press plays significant roles throughout. The salience of those roles is amplified by the press's role as transmitter of information to all other players.

New Roles for the Public in Presidential Selection

The public carry no formal decision-making role in Supreme Court confirmations. However, public opinion is the largely silent factor that hangs over the heads of elites in the judicial selection process.

Presidents know that their nominees must stand before the bar of public opinion and receive approval. Similarly, senators cannot ignore it because it may have implications on reelection and general constituency support. However, neither presidents nor senators usually acknowledge that public opinion carries any weight in their decision-making processes.

How have the public gained a toehold in Supreme Court appointments? As interest groups and the news media have entered the process, the public have, too. Interest groups have sought to mobilize the public in the nomination process to gain greater legitimacy for their involvement (i.e., speaking in the name of the people), as well as greater power to shape the outcome of the process.

The mobilization of the public has even turned lower federal court nominations, particularly controversial ones, into "constituency-driven events."[26] Supreme Court nominations today are high-profile news events with the potential of attracting the interest of a large segment of the American public. The opinions of the public about a nominee are considered of far greater importance today than previously.

Since the advent of scientific public opinion polling in the 1930s, this method has been used (even abused) in gauging public opinion on a wide range of national issues and events. But the Supreme Court nomination process rarely received much attention in polling until the 1980s.

Although public opinion surveys occasionally measured public attitudes about nominees previously, the Robert Bork nomination was the first to feature extensive use of the polls.[27] Today the public regularly is surveyed about favorable or unfavorable feelings toward nominees and even whether the nominee should be confirmed.

One of the drawbacks of the use of polling in Supreme Court confirmations is the widespread lack of public knowledge about the nominee for most nominations. For example, news coverage of Ruth Bader Ginsburg, which received front page and lead story prominence for only a couple of days following the announcement, dimmed from then on. Not surprisingly, 50 percent of the public admitted that they didn't know who Ruth Bader Ginsburg was, and 60 percent said they couldn't say anything about her ideology. Similarly, 60 percent said that of Breyer.[28] Surprisingly, polls during the Bork confirmation hearings showed the public had little knowledge of the qualifications of Robert Bork, even after several months of news coverage.[29] This may reflect the public's reluctance to place judgments on the qualifications of professionals, or it may indicate that little of the press coverage focuses on the nominee's qualifications but instead highlights conflict among elites.

Nevertheless, polls can become a salient part of a nomination process. Such surveys were frequent during the Bork and Thomas nominations but have also occurred during less controversial nominations, such as those for David Souter, Ruth Bader Ginsburg, and Stephen Breyer.[30] The salience of the public's opinion about the confirmation of a Supreme Court nominee is no longer seriously questioned.

Public opinion surveys then have become staples of Supreme Court confirmations. When elites are largely united in support of the nominee, polls become less important because public opinion reflects the lack of elite conflict. However, when elites are divided and interest groups use the news media to carry on their conflict with each other and the administration, the public can become involved but also divided over confirmation.

What exactly does public opinion do in the Supreme Court nomination process?

Tipping the Balance of Power

Public opinion plays a greater role in the outcome or the shape of the process in high-profile nominations when elites (the White House, senators, groups, the press) are at odds over confirmation. First, public interest is higher in contentious confirmation battles. For example, a July 1991 Times-Mirror News Interest survey, conducted long before the Anita Hill accusations, showed that 66 percent of respondents said they had followed the nomination of Clarence Thomas at least fairly closely.[31] In the midst of the Clarence Thomas–Anita Hill hearings, one survey suggested about 70 percent of Americans followed the hearings at least fairly closely.[32] According to a *New York Times* survey, 90 percent of people surveyed had watched at least part of the hearings.[33]

By contrast, the low-profile Ginsburg nomination in 1993, according to one survey, attracted less than half of Americans to pay at least fairly close attention to the news of her confirmation.[34] Other stories at the time—Midwest flooding and a controversy over homosexuals in the military—received more of the attention of the public.[35]

One reason for the lack of a public role with consensual appointments that have less controversy is the dearth of news coverage, which, in turn, occurs because of the absence of public conflict among elites. The deluge of group communication with the press slows to a trickle as opposition groups save their ammunition for more viable targets and supportive groups need not expend resources on a guaranteed outcome.

However, the potential for increased public attention is ever present, as indicated by the sudden upswing in public attention to the Thomas nomination once Anita Hill made her sexual harassment charges. A misstep by a nominee, a scandal allegation, or opposition from high-profile elites can trigger more news stories, more active group response, and greater public notice of a hitherto low-profile process. That potential cannot be ignored by players, and they must anticipate it in their decision-making calculus.

When a nomination is controversial and elites are divided, the public's response can become a tipping mechanism that provides leverage for one side or the other. To an extent unheard of in Supreme Court nominations, a plethora of polls appeared in the wake of the Thomas hearings. Survey respondents were queried not only whether Thomas should be confirmed but also on who was telling the truth—Thomas or Anita Hill. The public was expected to serve as judge of their veracity. According to two political scientists, ultimately the senators voting on Thomas deferred to public opinion.[36]

Helping Politicize the Nomination Process

Public opinion also can affect the traditional players' conduct of the process. For example, the public apparently has acquired greater acceptance of senators' exploration of a nominee's political views in questioning and decision making. Such license may encourage senators in an open search for the nominee's ideological views and the use of ideology as a criterion in voting on confirmation.[37]

This democratization of the appointment process is ironic, given the clear intent of the framers of the U.S. Constitution to exclude the public. Like the presidential selection process, the judicial selection process was constructed as an elite-driven process—that is, a president and a Senate removed from direct election by the public, appointing a Court similarly unlinked to the public.

Today, however, the other players recognize the necessity of gaining the public's support to obtain victory. Justification for the inclusion of the public in the confirmation process rests on the reality of the effects of Supreme Court action on the general public. Decisions of the Court have an impact on individuals' social relationships, business decisions, religious activity, and political roles.

Moreover, public involvement in this process is part of a trend of the increased public role in American political life, as mentioned earlier. The rise of electoral primaries, the reliance on public opinion surveys for gauging public will, and frequent reference to the salience of public opinion in policy decisions have provided the environment for the public to have a role in Supreme Court appointments as well.

Personalizing the Process

Moreover, there are aspects of Supreme Court nominations that foster a public role. Even though the public cannot judge the nominee's credentials as peers in the legal community (such as the ABA) do, other facets of this process invite a public role.

One is the emphasis on a particular individual. Unlike policy initiatives, Supreme Court nominations center on a particular person. The public need only assess a person, not bills or policy papers. In this sense, the judicial appointment process matches other selection systems that involve the public. In our weak party electoral system, candidates rather than party organizations become the focus of voter attention. Voters can approach a Supreme Court nominee much as they do a candidate for president or governor or even Congress. The task is even easier in a sense because only a single individual is involved and the response, plebiscite-like, need be only "yes" or "no."

Symbolizing the Process

Another public-friendly aspect is White House and group articulation of the appointment as symbols of current political conflicts. Elites make appointments relevant to the public by framing them in ways that the public can relate and respond to. For example, Sandra Day O'Connor and Ruth Bader Ginsburg became symbols of the role of women in society. Clarence Thomas was a representation of the struggle of African Americans to achieve political and social equality.

Of course, the White House is not the only purveyor of symbols designed to elicit public response. Senators and groups in opposition also do so. Senator Edward Kennedy's famous speech describing "Robert Bork's America" as a place where Americans would not want to live is an example.

Nor was Bork the only target. One year earlier, Kennedy had charged that William Rehnquist, then a nominee for chief justice, was "too extreme on race, too extreme on women's rights, too extreme on freedom of speech, too extreme on separation of church and state, too extreme to be chief justice."[38]

Kennedy's statements were designed to place Supreme Court nomination in the context of current social issues in order to mobilize public opinion. Nor was Kennedy unique. Richard Nixon's repeated line that he wanted judges who favored "peace forces" over "criminal forces" referred to the public's concern about crime and his own election theme of law and order.[39]

Failure to articulate a nomination in terms relevant to the public is an invitation to defeat. Robert Bork is a classic example. In the tradition of past judicial nominees, who spent little or no time in confirmation hearings or spoke primarily to legal elites, Bork provided lengthy, byzantine answers to senators' questions and seemed uncomfortable in the witness chair. (The fact that Bork was a chain smoker who could not indulge during his hours-long questioning may have enhanced his nervous appearance.) As a consequence, Bork wasted the opportunity to allay public fears about his nomination with answers pitched to an attentive television audience.

While much of the portrayal is policy oriented, it may be role oriented in the sense that groups define a justice's role in a certain way that resonates with the public.[40] For example, the strict constructionist theme used by several presidents reinforces the public view that judges should not substitute their own personal views for those in the Constitution. On the other hand, senators opposing Robert Bork claimed that he was "out of the mainstream" of judicial philosophy, which suggested that the role of the judge is to stay within a certain range of public acceptance of their jurisprudence.

Yet, the role-oriented framing clearly implies policy-oriented framing because words such as "strict constructionist" in the context of a particular era connote specific references to policy. For Nixon, it was the Court's decisions on obscenity, abortion, desegregation, rights of the accused, and a host of social policy issues. For Senator Kennedy, "out of the mainstream" was code for a right-wing extremist. Moreover, groups are less likely to use role framing because they need to communicate to supporters the specific benefit or harm a nominee will produce for their cause.

5

Today's Nomination Process

The Battle over Image

The new roles of external players have transformed the Supreme Court nomination process from an insider game dominated by the political interplay among the administration, senators, and, often, the legal community into one with a broader array of players, including interest groups (outside the legal community), the press, and the public. With this change, judicial selection has become a public process prone to the same emphases as other public selection processes such as elections and executive branch appointments—that is, image making to shape mass perceptions. As presidential campaigns seek to shape voters' images of a candidate, so Supreme Court nominations have become an attempt by the White House to secure certain perceptions of the nominee in the minds of elites and the public.

But just as the image of a candidate in an electoral race is contended over by competing campaigns (as well as by independent players such as the press and groups), so is the image-making process over a Supreme Court nominee a battle among various players. Who are these players and what do they do to shape the images of Supreme Court appointments?

White House Image Making

The primary (and typically initial) image maker is the White House. The times when the White House could offer a nominee and anticipate rapid, favorable confirmation by the Senate, sometimes within days, are over. The White House must sell the nominee to the other players, including groups, the press, and the public.

Such "selling" requires creating an image of a nominee. Because an image inevitably will form, the nominee and the White House want to be the first to shape it. As we will see later, failure to do so can result in a vacuum filled by other players, particularly groups and the press.

White House efforts in image making are not designed merely to aid the nominee. Their primary concern is the public's perception of the president. The nominee's image is a means to the end of shoring up the president's persona before voters. When confirmation is achieved, presidents seek to bask in the glory of their success, hoping it will stick to them and not just to the nominee.

For example, on the day his first Supreme Court justice was confirmed, President Clinton conducted a Rose Garden ceremony intended to allow him to take public credit for an administration success. Faced by a phalanx of reporters and cameras, the president used the photo opportunity to share the stage with his popular nominee. To assure that the press corps and the public did not miss the point, Clinton explicitly linked his success with his first Supreme Court appointment to Senate passage of a national service program and claimed that gridlock was over in the federal government.[1]

Similarly, when Judge Breyer's nomination was announced, the president took advantage of the positive reaction to Breyer's appointment by inviting the Massachusetts judge and his wife to spend the night at the White House the day before the ceremony and then jog with him the next morning. The next morning, television news cameras taped the new nominee and the president, jogging and conversing like old friends.

The White House image-making process starts even before the announcement of a nominee. The administration's release of names under consideration guarantees group, media, and Senate reaction. That reaction can be helpful in predicting confirmation chances before the president becomes committed to a certain nominee. Obviously, it becomes an opportunity for the press and groups to sabotage a nominee they oppose. Nixon knew this and sought to keep his choices out of public view. When he was on the verge of appointing two people to fill vacancies, Nixon told his chief of staff, H. R. Haldeman: "I don't want either of the people we're considering out in front. It's going to destroy them."[2]

Nixon was right. Once the American Bar Association leaked Nixon's short list, the press coverage was devastating. The *New York Times* reported that the husband of one potential nominee, Mildred Lillie, "had been sued 22 times in 10 years for non-payment of debt." One *New York Times* reporter wondered whether the president was trying to demean the Court with mediocre appointments. Opposition groups also piled on. The liberal Americans for Democratic Action dismissed Nixon's list as "a bewildering assortment of mediocrities," while the Reverend Jesse Jackson called them "racists and bigots."[3] None of those on the list received the nomination.

Another example occurred during the Clinton administration, when U.S. Appellate Judge Jon O. Newman was named as a prospective nominee. Although Newman was supported by some of the administration vetters (reportedly including White House Counsel Bernard Nussbaum), the release of his name resulted in a flood of negative reactions from conservative interest groups and Republican senators allied with them.

When President Nixon was seriously considering a woman and only floating the name of Senator Byrd, he directed his chief of staff, H. R. Haldeman, to leak information that the senator was at the top of the list but not the woman candidate: "Let whoever leaked out the fact that I was not considering Byrd leak out the fact a woman really doesn't have a chance, see what I mean? Let them float that out there, that actually the two top runners are two men."[4]

Presidents know that their image-making strategies can be ruined if others can set images first, hence the importance of establishing a frame for a nominee at the outset. This frame is the story of the nominee.

The Nominee's Story

In an era of symbolism, as mentioned at the end of the previous chapter, it is no surprise that Supreme Court nominee image making is primarily based on a symbolic story. The story defines the nominee in a way that enhances public appeal and makes confirmation more likely, because senators are unlikely to want to oppose a nominee with an alluring personal story. When nominees offer a story of themselves, the story is designed to appeal to certain stereotypes in American life.

The classic example of symbolic story was Clarence Thomas's. The Bush administration labored from the outset to create a highly positive public image of Clarence Thomas. Thomas's upbringing, with a strong, influential grandfather and his rise out of poverty, resonated with the public because it fit the American ideal. The Bush administration's "Pinpoint strategy" for Clarence Thomas (named after his hometown in Georgia) suggested a young man who emerged from poverty to recognized accomplishments, yet had not forgotten his roots.

Consequently, even though Thomas's accuser, Anita Hill, carried her own image of a sober, staid Oklahoma law school professor with no apparent motive for accusing a Supreme Court nominee, initial public opinion tilted toward Thomas.[5] To some extent, Thomas had been inoculated by his own image.

Nor was Thomas's image making an aberration. Ruth Bader Ginsburg's story focused on the gender discrimination she experienced in her early years and portrayed a woman who was oppressed by societal limitations but overcame them. Stephen Breyer talked about his youthful experiences as a ditchdigger.

Although none of these stories or incidents, on their own, was false, the image was not a total one. Clarence Thomas had long since abandoned the poverty of his youth. He had adopted a right-wing political ideology that, for obvious reasons, was not allowed to be part of the image presented to the general public. Ruth Bader Ginsburg had long since been accepted as part of the legal establishment and was even judged as somewhat conservative by the constituent groups who were expected to support her. And Stephen Breyer was primarily an academic whose real-world experiences were far more exceptions to his reality than the rule. Both Ginsburg and Breyer were wealthy individuals whose lives had been spent primarily in law schools or legal chambers.

Because the nominees' public life stories were not complete, they were not wholly accurate. Nevertheless, administrations extract from personal backgrounds those parts of the past that would be viewed as appealing to the general public. For example, in the case of Ruth Bader Ginsburg, the Clinton administration sought to channel press and public attention to her moderate judicial record to bolster the conclusion that she was a centrist acceptable to both parties. Her advocacy career was downplayed as uncontroversial. But it was that very period that became the battleground on image making by others, particularly opposition groups.

Why do nominees go through this transformation? The public nature of the process requires it. Because external players can weigh in on the fate of nominees, they want to be convinced that the individual embodies American democratic principles. Ideally, their life stories reflect the American dream—the ethnic whose ancestors came nearly penniless to American shores, the woman who overcomes gender discrimination, the African American who escapes poverty to achieve high political office. They become symbols for values and groups.[6]

Explicit story making is a fairly new tactic and has emerged because the White House had created a vacuum that allowed others to define the nominee. Robert Bork was not made appealing to the public by the Reagan administration. In fact, Bork was almost demonized by opposition interest groups and some press articles. For example, a *Time* magazine cover story showed Bork dressed in black with the headline "Bork: How a young socialist became a conservative and one of history's most controversial Supreme Court nominees." Within the story, one photograph displayed a young Bork holding a snake with the caption "his intellectual odyssey 'departs from the conventional.'"[7]

Bork's experience was ironic, given the Reagan White House's previous success with the president's own image. In fairness, Bork was committed to the notion that the confirmation process was primarily an intellectual exercise, and he may not have cooperated, as much as was necessary, in White House image-making efforts. Nevertheless, when opposition mounted, there was no reservoir of public goodwill, no public acceptance of Bork as a person that offered a benefit of the doubt to the nominee.

The Reagan administration and Judge Robert Bork made the mistake of allowing opposing groups and the press to define the nominee's story. Rather than the image of a thoughtful conservative academic and jurist, as the White House expected him to be portrayed naturally, Bork became a wild-eyed radical who lacked understanding of the real world and the effects of his legal views on everyday people. His public persona fed the story. His unshaped beard and frizzy hair, coupled with an academic's approach to senators' questions, confirmed the veracity of the image others assigned him.

Subsequent White House image makers learned important lessons from the Bork defeat. When President George H. W. Bush nominated New Hampshire federal judge David Souter to replace Justice William Brennan, the White House quickly portrayed Souter as a stereotypical New Englander with old-fashioned American values. The process was repeated the next year when Clarence Thomas was nominated to succeed Justice Thurgood Marshall. Thomas became the embodiment of the American dream of the poor African American child who grows up to attend Yale, serve in positions in the executive branch, and take an appointment on the U.S. Supreme Court.

The "story" nominations have included Antonin Scalia (first Italian American), Clarence Thomas (second African American and embodiment of rags to riches and specifically the success of efforts to assist African Americans out of poverty), and Ruth Bader Ginsburg (second woman and a long-time advocate for women's rights). All of these individuals achieved confirmation and, in the case of Thomas, even received public support against strong opposition to confirmation.

Other nominees have not had a strong "story," and then image making becomes more problematic for the White House. These are "stealth" nominees who lack a story, yet they also lack definable records that would engender opposition. Recent "stealth" nominees include Anthony Kennedy and David Souter.

One exception was Stephen Breyer. Breyer was not a stealth candidate because he was well known in the judicial community, with a long record of judicial behavior. However, he lacked the compelling life drama other "story" nominees possessed. Hence, he attempted to create a story of real-world exposure by relating his ditchdigger experience, thus reassuring the public he was a man who understood the problems of ordinary people. But the moderate Breyer's reservoir of bipartisan support within the Judiciary Committee may have overcome the lack of story or stealth.

Unlike Breyer, nominees who lack the "story" and whose views on a range of issues are widely known, such as Robert Bork and William Rehnquist, typically face challenges in winning confirmation. Presidents who ignore the need for a "story" or appoint those with well-known ideological views do so at their own peril.

The story or stealth routes work best when the nominee is little known to the public in advance. Why? Image making is easier with a blank slate.

Supreme Court appointments are well designed for image making because nominations often begin with that blank slate in terms of public awareness of the nominee. Over more than 200 years, few Supreme Court nominees have been widely known to the public when they were nominated. And even that rare level of familiarity to the public has been nonexistent in recent years.[8]

Well-known figures, however, particularly politicians, already have public records that make image making difficult. For example, although President Clinton wanted to appoint a politician to the Court, shaping the image of that individual would have been much more difficult than doing so for a lesser known individual. Clinton encountered some of that difficulty when he publicly considered Bruce Babbitt, former Arizona governor, 1988 Democratic presidential candidate, and then Interior secretary. Floating Babbitt's name led to immediate opposition from conservatives. As mentioned in chapter 2, it is no coincidence that elected officials, with their strong name recognition and public and controversial records, have been passed over for nomination since Earl Warren.

Federal appellate judges, on the other hand, are particularly advantaged in this process in that they rarely carry a public image that needs to be changed.[9] Instead, images can be made from scratch.

Meeting Public Expectations

The White House needs the nominee to appear to correspond to public expectations of a Supreme Court justice. The public imagines justices as fair-minded individuals who act like the symbol of justice, with its blind approach to arbitrating disputes in society. Therefore, Supreme Court justices are supposed to be jurists or legal thinkers who carry no specific agendas with them as they ascend the bench. Justices are not supposed to be ideological extremists who use the bench to further their own ideology.

Conveying that message about the nominee embodies knowledge that the public is critical to the administration's success in winning elite and public support and eventual confirmation. For example, in 1993 the Clinton administration quickly sought to depict the nomination of Ruth Bader Ginsburg as consistent with the centrist, nonideological tone of the Clinton administration. The administration's line, repeated over and over, was that Ruth Bader Ginsburg, like Bill Clinton, was a centrist who eschewed ideological labels. Judge Ginsburg herself reinforced that image with her subsequent public comments.

However, the success of the Ginsburg nomination was not repeated initially in the next nomination. In a session with the press immediately after the announcement, White House Counsel Lloyd Cutler described Breyer as "the one who had the fewest problems."[10] Rather than personifying the ideals of the judicial system, the appointment was inadvertently portrayed as the outcome of a nakedly political process in which the least objectionable candidate is the winner.

An important aspect of image making is to minimize the appearance of political factors in the selection process. Presidents present nominees to the public with the inevitable line that this person deserves the position almost wholly because of merit and that regardless of the constituency nature of the appointment, once the credentials of the individual are known, there will be consensus on granting confirmation.

President George H. W. Bush's declaration, mentioned earlier, that Clarence Thomas was "the best person for this position" is one example.[11] Similarly, President Clinton's anger during the Ginsburg press conference at the insinuation that politics played a role in his decision making rather than just merit is another piece of evidence of the critical nature of framing the appointment for the press and the public as apolitical.

Meeting Supporter Expectations

The mass public is not the only attentive audience. Perhaps an even more attuned one is the administration's supporters within the electorate. Through image making, presidents also need to signal to their supporters that their picks, particularly consensual ones, reflect the president's ideological direction and therefore serve their constituency. One example is President Reagan's announcement that the individuals he chose were "attentive to the rights specifically guaranteed in our Constitution and the proper role of the courts in our democratic system."[12] In a specific instance, when Sandra Day O'Connor was nominated by Reagan, the White House reiterated the claim that O'Connor shared Reagan's views on social issues of the day, such as school busing, abortion, and the death penalty.[13]

Another related, vital message from the White House that is often directed specifically at supporters is a thematic element to the appointment. Since Richard Nixon, presidents have defined their Supreme Court appointments through themes. For Nixon it was "strict constructionism." Ronald Reagan and George Bush promised to appoint justices who would not legislate from the bench.

Similarly, President Clinton communicated his desire to find a nominee who would have a "big heart." One aide said the president wanted a candidate much like Thurgood Marshall, who could bring a "moral dimension" to the law.[14] The mention of Thurgood Marshall and "big heart" suggested that the president would appoint a liberal, thus satisfying the left wing of the Democratic Party.

Groups and Images

The White House rarely engages in image making alone. Groups also attempt to shape the public image of the nominee. And that effort almost always is undertaken to contradict the administration's image.

As mentioned earlier, while the White House sought to portray Robert Bork as a moderately conservative justice in the judicial mainstream, opponents pressed a different image—one of a wild-eyed radical beyond the pale of American judicial thought. One anti-Bork ad even featured Gregory Peck, the popular actor with moral authority from his famous portrayal of lawyer Atticus Finch in *To Kill A Mockingbird*, standing in front of the Supreme Court building as he warned of the dangers of a Bork appointment. Although the ad actually appeared only once, news coverage carried the ad's message across the nation.[15]

The battle over competing images dominates the confirmation period. While the White House seeks to promote its image of the nominee, opposition groups offer the public a contrasting view. For example, David Souter's confirmation process was a struggle between the White House–sponsored image of a solid New Englander with an open mind versus the opposition's portrayal of a monastic loner who had little contact with real-world social problems.

The White House carries the advantage of surprise in image making. While the administration knows who the nominee will be and can begin to construct a public image, opposition groups are operating in the dark about exactly who will be the nominee until a formal announcement is made. The fact that the White House initiates the public image campaign with the announcement of the nominee and therefore gets to set the first public impressions aids the White House in the struggle over image. The announcement usually is the commencement of the image-making campaign. For example, when Clarence Thomas was nominated, the accompanying statement the White House issued emphasized Thomas's roots in the small town of Pinpoint, Georgia, thus inaugurating the strategy to link Thomas to American values.

Opposing groups, then, must mobilize quickly to blunt the White House image campaign. In fact, that effort must occur during the first news cycle when the nomination is announced. Groups immediately offer their leaders for interviews and issue press releases designed to blunt the White House's image. Because groups rarely have the information prepared to deluge the press with opposition data, the best groups can do is question the White House image to delay any rush to judgment.

This effort is made easier by the nomination of well-known candidates whose names have circulated widely among the legal community. For example, liberal advocacy groups long counted on Robert Bork's nomination by the Reagan administration. Administration insiders acknowledged that Bork had come close to receiving the nomination just the year before he was nominated. Bork had even been on Gerald Ford's short list in 1975, when John Paul Stevens was nominated.

Hence, the opposition to Bork was prepared with extensive research to dull the White House image quickly. To blunt the effect of the White House image in press coverage and stop the usual rush to support by senators, within an hour of the White House announcement, Senator Edward Kennedy stood on the floor of the Senate and announced his opposition to Bork. Kennedy delivered a now famous speech decrying Robert Bork's America as one where "women would be forced into back alley abortions, blacks would sit at segregated lunch counters, rogue policemen could break down citizens' doors in midnight raids, school children could not be taught about evolution, writers and artists could be censured at the whim of government."[16]

Kennedy, in league with opposition groups, effectively signaled to other senators, the interest group community, the press, and the public that there should be no presumption of confirmation on the part of possible opposition forces. Because Bork was defeated in his confirmation bid, Kennedy's action became a model for creating an opposing image of a nominee quickly and effectively.

However, the Kennedy model is not universally applicable. When presidents nominate stealth candidates, they cannot so easily be labeled. A surprise nominee who is little known can catch groups off-guard. In those cases, groups have scanty evidence to bolster their contrasting image, and the White House image goes unchallenged.

The classic recent example is David Souter, who was little known even to legal groups, leading to an inability to counter the administration rapidly.[17] Clearly, Souter was a cipher in the judicial community. In stark contrast to Robert Bork, who had authored numerous opinions, articles, and books on current legal topics, Souter had never authored a book and had written only one law review article. Moreover, he had no record as a federal judge, having just been appointed three months earlier and having not written a single opinion before being nominated to the Supreme Court.[18]

Interestingly, it is not just opposition groups who seek to shape the nominee's image; groups generally supportive of the White House do so as well. For example, a pro–Clarence Thomas group placed an ad in the *Washington Post* featuring a photograph of poor black children. The ad reinforced the White House's Pinpoint strategy in selling Thomas to the nation.[19]

These groups may convey the image that the individual is more acceptable to the group's constituents than the White House image suggests. For example, when Ruth Bader Ginsburg was nominated in 1993, liberal groups sought to emphasize the parts of Ginsburg's record they agreed with to telegraph to their supporters how Ginsburg should be portrayed. The groups sought to describe Ginsburg as a liberal, not a centrist. The Alliance for Justice, for example, issued a report that described Ginsburg's record as "complex" and then detailed her decisions in several areas supporting liberal positions.

The liberal group concluded that her rulings as an appellate judge, which could be construed as centrist, if not conservative, had been constrained by conservative Supreme Court rulings Ginsburg needed to uphold. Rather, it was "the battles she fought prior to her service on the bench that portend a Justice who will broker the promises of the Constitution into reality."[20] Overall, the report attempted to find common ground with Ginsburg in areas important to the political left. The group was attempting to mold the public image of Ginsburg as more liberal than her judicial record would indicate.

However, such image making by supportive groups can be harmful to the White House's carefully crafted efforts. These groups may seek to further a more extreme image that promotes the group's interests, but they also may signal undecided senators that the nominee is not what the White House suggests.

Why do supportive groups seek to construct their own images of the nominee, even to the detriment of the White House? Image making on the part of groups is not geared exclusively to the general public. The primary intended recipients are group supporters. Image making by groups is designed to justify group support for a nominee who otherwise may be portrayed as only tepidly supportive of group interests. The separate image also reassures group constituents that the group has been successful in obtaining a nominee to the membership's liking. It enhances the image of the group as an influential player in nomination politics.

The battle is joined: Groups use the nomination to enhance their own position among the panoply of groups while the White House seeks to reinforce an image favorable to its own interests. One example was the fight over Stephen Breyer's image in 1994. Opposition groups and some columnists described Breyer not as a broad judicial thinker who belonged on the highest court in the land but as merely a technocrat. A *Washington Post* column quoted an attorney who pinpointed Breyer's potential image problem: "Judge Breyer, the legal technician, has helped create a finely tuned watch that is a mechanical wonder in its smooth and logical operations. The only problem is that, in the real world, it fails to keep time." But from the White House ceremony to the Senate committee hearing testimony, the White House and Breyer worked hard to blunt that characterization by adopting and repeating a catchy phrase "making law work for people" and promising that if Breyer was confirmed he would "remember that the decisions I help to make will have an effect upon the lives of many, many Americans."[21]

Using the Press for Image Making

When Richard Nixon nominated Lewis Powell and William Rehnquist to the Supreme Court in 1972, he appeared live on network prime-time television. Nixon bypassed the press. However, Nixon's approach was highly unusual and probably could not be duplicated today at a time when presidents find it difficult to get networks to break away from regular programming to cover presidential addresses other than State of the Union speeches. Before and since Nixon, presidents have relied on White House announcements, and increasingly ceremonies, outside of prime-time television to reveal the president's selection.

The image-making strategies of both the White House and groups—whether in support or opposition—hinge on the reception of the press to image-oriented messages. Yet, that reliance is affected by other factors, often unrelated to the goals of each player.

In utilizing the press, for example, the president carries distinct advantages. Not only does the White House's view usually come first, in that it becomes the first presented to the press and the public, but also the president is guaranteed press attention. Groups, however, have to compete for it.

Nevertheless, the administration's intended image can be damaged by negative press coverage based on a poorly conducted selection process or the emergence of information the White House conveniently omitted or failed to find. An example of the former was the Clinton administration's attempt to replace Justice Byron White in 1993. White resigned in March, giving the administration ample time to conduct the selection process, make an announcement, and still give the Senate several months for the confirmation stage—all before the August recess of the Congress. But the administration seemed to squander the time White had given them when the president still had not decided on a nominee nearly three months after White's retirement announcement. The press's expectations of a speedy process were based on Reagan and Bush's quick announcements. *Baltimore Sun* White House correspondent Carl Cannon later explained press reaction to the nomination process: "The problem is that this process had simply gone on so long, that Clinton was beginning to look inept. In fact, it was past the point of beginning to look inept. Because he had had all of these other problems with nominees, people were writing the stories hard."[22]

Even worse for the Clinton administration, delays in decision making after repeated promises that an announcement was forthcoming damaged the administration's credibility with the press. Absent those assured deadlines, the press probably would have not drawn the conclusion that the administration's process was so chaotic.

Moreover, the White House's efforts to shape the press's portrayal of the selection process do not occur within a vacuum. General conflicts with the press over access to administration officials and reliable information spill over into the Supreme Court selection process, as it does into every other point of contact between the White House and the press. A White House enmeshed in conflict with the press may engender negative coverage of a Supreme Court nomination as well.

That also means image making to cultivate a press portrayal of a successful nomination also may be perceived through the lens of press perception of the current administration. By 1987, President Reagan was perceived widely as a weakened lame-duck president. His administration had become enmeshed in the Iran-contra scandal. Robert Bork's nomination came in the midst of that perception of vulnerability.

Not only political factors but also the reality of news professionals' own imperatives in approaching news are critical in the role of the press in the image-making process. Events with news values elicit the concentrated interest of journalists. Conversely, events lacking conflict and drama are less compelling. The Clinton administration suffered from this comparison when Ruth Bader Ginsburg was nominated in 1993. Her nomination came in the wake of the intensely newsworthy Clarence Thomas nomination. Press reaction seemed to reflect disappointment that the confirmation process would be placid, as opposed to the excitement of both Thomas and, earlier, Bork. One reporter commented that the Ginsburg nomination was not typical because it had "no juice."[23] The confirmation process lacked the drama and excitement reporters had come to expect. But the press frustration also was just another means to criticize a president unpopular with the press and perceived as disliked by the public as well.

Obviously, the White House is not the only attempted user of news media to relay messages to other players in the process. Other frequent users are members of the Senate, particularly those who serve on the Senate Judiciary Committee. Their objective is to serve individual or institutional goals in the process.

The classic example is the effort of the Senate Judiciary Committee to restore its reputation in the wake of the Thomas hearings in 1991. The committee sought to transmit the message that the next hearing would be much different from the preceding one. The inclusion of a closed session to air personal issues had the potential of allowing the Senate to resolve some issues without publicly discrediting either the nominee or the Senate. However, one scholar argues that the process of privatizing Senate Judiciary Committee sessions "tends to shield senators from accountability to the voters and deprives interest groups and individual citizens of information that is relevant to their intelligent participation in the judicial selection process."[24]

In 1993 and 1994, the Judiciary Committee was successful in avoiding the disaster it had experienced in 1991, at least partly because of the absence of damaging personal accusations concerning the next nominees. However, the committee did not escape unscathed. In the Ginsburg and Breyer confirmation hearings, members were panned by the press as the intellectual subordinates of the nominees.

Nevertheless, that criticism was preferable to an image of a committee wallowing in a discussion of sordid personal matters or displaying hostility toward women. Generally, the Senate was successful in achieving the objective of avoiding a public relations disaster, even if it could not elevate its overall reputation through the process.

Individual senators also use the press to send messages to the White House. As mentioned earlier, Democratic senators during the George W. Bush administration offered to work with the president on a Supreme Court nominee to encourage a centrist candidate. How-ever, Republican senators used the press to communicate the opposite message, urging the White House to ignore the Democrats.[25]

Senate attempts to exploit press coverage to intervene publicly in presidential selection are most intense when the decision-making process is nearing completion. For example, in the midst of the final stages of White House decision making in 1993 between Babbitt and Breyer, Senator Biden told reporters he felt Breyer would be easier to confirm. Similarly, through an unusual weekend press release, Sena-tor Kennedy made a last-ditch public effort that same year to defuse Breyer's Social Security tax payment problem and urge the White House to nominate the Massachusetts judge.

Similarly, press coverage is essential to groups' efforts in the battle over image. As mentioned earlier, when an announcement is made, groups are quick to turn to the press for attention to their take on the nominee. In addition, groups issue reports on the nominee's background and record of jurisprudence that are designed to reinforce the impression they want the public to have of the new nominee. For example, after the nomination of Ruth Bader Ginsburg, the conserva-tive Family Research Council issued a report to senators and the press highlighting Ginsburg's role as a feminist advocate in the 1970s and questioning Ginsburg's centrist credentials that the Clinton admin-istration strongly touted. Similarly, the Judicial Monitoring Project of the Free Congress Foundation, a right-wing think tank, issued two treatises reviewing Ginsburg's legal philosophy and judging style, similarly concluding that she was more liberal than centrist.

These reports probably do not convert many senators in and of themselves. But they do signal an attempt to shake the White House's image-making campaign in the minds of other players, including other groups, the news media, and the public. And if these reports are coupled with other tactics such as intense grassroots lobbying, press conferences and releases, the construction of broad group coalitions, and even advocacy advertising, senators are likely to pay attention.

Reports are one of several tactics groups use to obtain coverage of their position on the nominee. A major media-focused opposition campaign through radio spots, news conferences, and news releases has become common. For example, the Bork opposition coalition bought advertising time in both print and broadcast media.[26]

Another form of group influence on the press is the op-ed column. Groups pressure editorial page editors to print their views on prospective nominee criteria in op-ed columns. Op-eds may be the work of group leaders who are advertising the group's position, or they may be written by "neutral" scholars who are enlisted by the group but whose affiliation remains unstated and therefore is unknown to the reader. Either way, once op-eds favorable to the group's position are published, the group packages them and sends them on to other media outlets to prove media support for the group's stance.[27]

Journalists have accorded groups a public legitimacy as affected parties by using them as sources. The relationship is symbiotic, as both members of the press and interest group representatives gain from the interaction. The former acquires information about prospective nominees and the nature of reaction to the nominee, and the groups see their views reflected in press coverage of the process.

In fact, particular groups have acquired a recognized status as news sources in coverage of the process. Table 5.1 lists the top ten specific organizations represented in nomination news in the *New York Times* and *Time* magazine from 1981 to 1993. Groups such as NARAL, the NAACP, the Leadership Conference on Civil Rights, and NOW have become essential sources for lists of potential nominees or reaction to nominees proposed by others.

Almost all of the top ten mentioned groups were opposed to the Reagan and Bush administration nominees. The only exceptions were the American Bar Association and National Right to Life. The ABA

Table 5.1
Top Ten Group Mentions in News Coverage of Supreme Court
Nominations 1981–1993

	New York Times	Time	ABC News
NARAL	16	5	10
NAACP	18	5	4
NOW	15	4	5
Leadership Conference on Civil Rights	12	8	4
National Right to Life	11	1	3
ABA	12	1	1
People for the American Way	10	2	2
ACLU	7	3	2
Alliance for Justice	7	2	1
Planned Parenthood	7	–	3

represents a different aspect because it has acquired a quasi-official role in the confirmation process and it does not actively lobby for or against nominees.

The dominance of liberal or left-leaning groups is due to their role in carrying the opposition to Reagan and Bush nominees. News stories usually contrasted opposing groups with the administration rather than with supportive groups. During this period, National Right to Life was most visible in opposition to Sandra Day O'Connor's nomination in 1981.

However, even potentially supportive groups are frequent sources for press stories. Liberal and women's groups have hardly been shy in using press coverage to state their positions on prospective nominees, even while favorable administrations held office.

The presence of interest groups does not necessarily equate with conflict. The O'Connor nomination elicited high-interest group involvement, but even opponents were somewhat muted, given their position of alliance with the Reagan administration and the failure of Republican senators (who controlled the Senate) to join the opposition. Ultimately, O'Connor was confirmed without a single opposition vote.

Perhaps a more accurate measure of the nature of conflict is the presence of opposition to the nominee or proposed nominee in the news story. That presence can be counted through the frequency of references to sources (groups, legal scholars, public officials) that oppose a nominee or proposed nominee.

The bias of sources toward nominees or (primarily in the case of the Ruth Bader Ginsburg nomination) potential nominees is represented in Table 5.2. Sources included not only group representatives but also legal scholars, members of the Senate, officials in the administration, and any others who were cited in nomination stories.

In terms of conflict, as represented by the bias of news sources, the change toward greater opposition occurred first with the Rehnquist nomination, where opposition sources far outnumbered supporters. With the verbal fire of various groups directed at Rehnquist, Scalia received both little attention and little opposition.

Even the relatively placid Souter nomination, which drew little opposition within the Senate, featured a decidedly mixed response as measured by the source mentions. Souter's confirmation was opposed by several prominent groups, such as NOW and NARAL.

The stories described in Table 5.2 covered the elongated presidential selection stage and not just the confirmation stage. Therefore, the opposition shown in the Ginsburg nomination process included those opposed not only to Ginsburg but also to potential nominees Bruce Babbitt and Stephen Breyer.

Obviously, the news media became a major player in the image-making process. To a great extent, the news media, because of their role as the linking mechanism, are the object of other players' efforts. The objective of conveying a certain image to other players and the public is achievable only with the cooperation of the press.

Yet, the news media can act as more than just a conduit for other players' image-making efforts. They also conduct investigative research to find holes in the administration's image. These may be personal in nature, as mentioned earlier, or they may relate to the nominee's official duties. For example, in 1994 a reporter for *Newsday* reported a case of potential conflict of interest involving a judicial deci-

Table 5.2
Direction of Source Statements in *New York Times* Supreme Court
Nomination Stories

	Support %	Oppose %	Neither %	Don't know %	Total %	Number of sources
Stewart/O'Connor	70	25	2	3	100	(61)*
Burger/Rehnquist	34	63	3	0	100	(73)
Scalia	60	30	10	0	100	(20)
Powell/Bork	45	47	8	0	100	(71)
Powell/Ginsburg	0	0	0	0	100	(0)
Powell/Kennedy	100	0	0	0	100	(10)
Brennan/Souter	43	45	10	2	100	(84)
Marshall/Thomas	39	59	2	0	100	(61)
White/Ginsburg	56	38	6	0	100	(34)

*number of sources included, not the number of stories

sion by Judge Breyer benefiting Lloyd's of London at the same time
he held investments that could be enhanced by the decision. However,
other news media did not pick up the story. The *New York Times* and
the *Washington Post* did not perceive the issue as an important ethical
breach, thus limiting the story's impact.

News media also make editorial judgments that may affect the
image-making process. Initial editorial judgments can signal to other
players, particularly the attentive public, how the press views nominees and whether the press will engage in support or opposition to
confirmation of the nominee.

Several messages can be carried in editorial judgments. One is
the merit of the president's selection. For example, editorial reaction to Judge Ginsburg's appointment included glowing praise of her.
The *New York Times* termed her "an excellent choice for the high
court." The *Washington Post* announced that news of her appointment was received with "enthusiasm and confidence that the honor
was deserved."

However, President Nixon's announcement of G. Harrold Carswell
in 1970 provoked criticism of the mediocrity of the appointment. The

New York Times editorialized that Carswell was "so totally lacking in professional distinction, so wholly unknown for cogent opinions or learned writings, that the appointment is a shock. It almost suggests an intention to reduce the significance of the Court by lowering the caliber of its membership."[28]

Another is a message about the inevitability of the success of confirmation. For example, following President Lyndon Johnson's nomination of Justice Abe Fortas as chief justice, press coverage exhibited a sense of inevitability about the appointment. The *New York Times* copy read as if Fortas was a shoo-in for confirmation and Johnson's choice was tantamount to taking the oath of office.[29] For the first time, however, the prediction of inevitability was mistaken. The supportive editorial failed to deter the opposition, which successfully blocked the nomination until Fortas withdrew his name from consideration.

Still a third message concerns the nature of the Senate's process in reaching judgment. Press intervention can help legitimate Senate and perhaps even public acceptance of Senate assertiveness. When Judge Bork was nominated in 1987, the *New York Times* editorialized that a judge's philosophy was fair game for Senate inquiry and that the Senate was justified in ascertaining a nominee's views on issues such as abortion and the First Amendment.[30]

The Importance of Image

The battle over the nominee's image is one with direct consequences for confirmation. Whether the nominee becomes an appealing individual to the public or a pariah is determined through the battle over image. Image making determines confirmation success, which explains the critical nature of the battle over the public image. Robert Bork lost the battle for elite and public support because his image contrasted with that expected for Supreme Court justices. Others have won because the administration, usually with the help of external forces, succeeded in conveying an appealing image balancing humanness and appropriate judicial temperament.

The nominee's image is not the only one at stake. The images of all other players are affected by the outcome of the process or even by the process itself. As mentioned earlier, the president's image is very much at stake. The White House's success or failure in the nomination process can spill over into other areas of presidential leadership.

One of the objectives of a particular Supreme Court nomination can be boosting public approval of the president to aid the president in achieving other goals. For example, President Clinton was in the midst of a public opinion free fall when the Ginsburg nomination was announced in 1993. The immediate effect was a temporary halt in that free fall.

The use of Supreme Court appointments to affect public opinion toward the president is problematic, however. Public opinion spill-over from Supreme Court appointments seems to work at best as a neutral factor and often as a negative one. Presidents do not gain public support from consensual nominees because news coverage diminishes and a significant portion of the public remains largely unaware of the presence of the nominee and the process. As would be expected from such a low-profile event as an uncontroversial Supreme Court appointment, there is no long-term approval gain for the president.

A high-profile nominee, on the other hand, attracts press notice and public attention but is more likely to harm the president because of the controversy engendered by the appointment. For example, by appointing Clarence Thomas to the court, President George H. W. Bush may have succeeded in satisfying some conservative groups. But Bush's public approval ratings continued to fall as he faced a primary challenge for reelection.

In fact, failure to confirm a nominee can reinforce the image of an ineffectual president. The Reagan administration's inability to confirm Robert Bork reinforced the image of Reagan as a lame-duck president. Failure instills in others a sense of the administration's weakness; success may result in temporary goodwill but primarily relief over the absence of failure. Supreme Court nominations bring few spillover benefits to presidential approval, but they can be abundant with draw-backs for an administration.

To avoid such damage, administrations sometimes distance them-selves from unpopular nominees. Again, the Bork process is a clas-sic example. While Robert Bork struggled to gain confirmation in the face of widespread opposition from groups and, eventually, a majority of senators, the Reagan administration backed away from active sup-port. In contrast, the Bush administration worked actively in Clarence Thomas's behalf, even in the midst of his difficulties. But this action, at the commencement of the president's reelection bid, was a contributing factor to his subsequent free fall in the public opinion polls (although not necessarily with his own core constituency) and eventual defeat.

Others' images are also at stake. The groups who stake out posi-tions and engage in active support or opposition are affected. For example, in the Ginsburg nomination, women's groups, concerned about their image with the press and their own constituency, did not want to be seen publicly opposing a female nominee. They would face stronger approbation than some of the African American leadership faced when opposing Clarence Thomas on account of Ginsburg's past activity as a leader in the women's movement. Hence, although many group leaders worried about Ginsburg's views, they offered at least tepid support during the confirmation process.

Even opposition groups have their own image-making efforts in mind. In the Ginsburg nomination, for example, conservative groups, who faced certain defeat in an effort to derail the Ginsburg confirma-tion process, still needed to satisfy constituents that they performed a useful function in the judicial selection.

The opposition's focus in such circumstances is on the future. Speaking during the Ginsburg confirmation process in 1993, Thomas Jipping claimed the conservative camp still gained mileage during the confirmation process from their efforts opposing Ginsburg: "We are using the Ginsburg nomination, not so much to lobby against her. . . . But we're using this as a way of defining these issues, of activism and restraint. . . . Getting on the record the way we evaluate judges; using it as a kind of educational effort for the future."[31]

When opposition is politically doomed, the groups walk a fine line. On one hand, their constituencies expect some action will be taken to express their views. On the other hand, the group does not want to waste political capital on a fruitless effort. Rather, they prefer to save their ammunition for more effective fights.

In addition, the groups' other battles may affect the Senate's willingness to engage a nominee likely to win confirmation anyway. In 1986, liberal groups fought the nomination of William Rehnquist as chief justice and spent their political capital on that effort. But after Rehnquist won confirmation, Democrats in the Senate had no appetite for further controversy and essentially acquiesced in the confirmation of Antonin Scalia to replace Rehnquist, giving liberal groups little opportunity for organized opposition.[32]

However, image making by external forces, particularly groups, is fraught with potential dangers for the legitimacy of the process. Because groups are intent on using nominations to further group goals, communications with constituencies about nominees can be subject to distortions. Such distortions further a group's aims of justifying group support or opposition, as well as of mobilizing the constituencies to action. Even Justice Ginsburg herself, while an appellate judge, commented on this problem. She confessed that she had "no magic formula for making the interest groups involved act more responsible, for keeping their comment fair."[33]

Similarly, utilizing the press as the medium for image making carries inherent biases. The press's own imperatives must be met, transforming the selection process into a public campaign that meets news values.

External Players and the Process

With the inclusion of these other external players, Supreme Court nominations are hardly isolated events in American life. They fit into the whole fabric of political and even social activity. The events of a Supreme Court nomination process have had a spillover effect into other aspects of American life affecting the public. For example, the Thomas nomination provided new impetus to a national discussion over the issue of sexual harassment in the workplace.[34]

The electoral process also has been affected. Since the 1980s, presidential campaigns have featured debates over who would control the direction of the Supreme Court. In 1984, Walter Mondale predicted that if President Reagan were reelected, Moral Majority leader Reverend Jerry Falwell would choose Supreme Court nominees.[35] Similarly, in 1992 candidate Bill Clinton suggested that the nomination of Clarence Thomas was a mistake he would not commit if elected president. In the 2000 campaign, Vice President Al Gore claimed that Governor Bush as president would select justices who would overturn *Roe v. Wade*.[36] To show how he would save the Court, Gore's speeches included the line: "If you believe in a woman's right to choose—a right that must never be undermined, must never be weakened, must never be taken away—then join us now. The Supreme Court is at stake—and our campaign is your cause."[37]

Candidate George W. Bush promised in 2000 that he would appoint strict constructionists to the bench and not liberal activists.[38] In 2003, Democratic presidential nominee Senator John Kerry stated his view of the possible future of the Court if Bush was reelected:

> Just think what is at stake if President Bush is reelected for a second term and has the opportunity to appoint a Bush Majority on the Supreme Court. It could mean:
> - The end of affirmative action and a retreat from diversity in universities and workplaces
> - The end of *Roe v. Wade* and a woman's right to choose
> - A return to the criminalization of homosexuality
> - A threat to the federal government's ability to protect our air and water
> - A license to John Ashcroft to trample on our civil rights and invade our privacy
> - A weakening of the protections for ordinary American workers

- A threat to the rights of the disabled and the elderly
- A threat to the rights of African-American voters.[39]

Even a Supreme Court justice jumped into the fray at one point. In 1988, Justice Harry Blackmun explicitly linked nominations and elections when he commented that if Republicans won that presidential election, the Court could become "very conservative well into the twenty-first century."[40]

A Supreme Court nomination also helped mobilize a group of candidates. The Thomas nomination was widely viewed as helping launch the "Year of the Woman" and aiding women candidates in the 1992 elections.[41] One classic example was the defeat of Senator Alan Dixon by Carol Moseley Braun in the Illinois Democratic primary just five months after the Thomas confirmation vote. A major campaign theme by Moseley Braun was Dixon's vote in support of Thomas.

As this discussion has demonstrated, Supreme Court nominations affect not only the Court but also other players who have become involved—the president, the Senate, the nominees, related groups, and the news media. Because all have been drawn into the process, they are strongly motivated to emerge at the other end without damage to their respective positions, and perhaps become even stronger vis-à-vis other players.

Future Nominations

The potential for external force involvement has not diminished over time. Media coverage and interest group concern, as well as capability to influence the process, still exist as potential factors in the conduct of the nomination process.

The capability for media coverage of nominations has not changed. CNN and C-SPAN continue their policies of covering live, or on a delayed basis, events considered of great import to national policy, such as congressional hearings. With the creation of Court TV, a channel devoted to courtroom coverage, the options for nomination coverage have even been expanded.

Since the Bork and Thomas nominations, each new appointment carries the potential for high drama produced by conflict between the president and the Senate, Democrats and Republicans, and opposing interest groups. Moreover, the drama may be accentuated by scandal revealed by the investigative research conducted by these groups and by the press itself. Because few nominees already possess high name recognition among the public, the role of the press in introducing the individual to the public produces a plethora of personality pieces, as well as the opportunity for image shaping.

Interest groups are continually poised for involvement in nominations. Groups such as the Alliance for Justice, the Women's Legal Defense Fund, the National Organization for Women, and the National Abortion Rights Action League on the left and National Right to Life, Americans United for Life, Family Research Council, and Concerned Women for America on the right are no less capable of mobilizing than in the past. Moreover, as discussed previously, recently they have acted aggressively even in confirmations of lower court judges.

Public attention to the Court predicts public involvement in the nomination process. Decisions of the Court remain of interest to the public. The *Bush v. Gore* case was closely followed, understandably. But other cases also have acquired public attention in areas such as flag burning, abortion, right to die, and school vouchers.[42]

The stage is set for continued external player involvement in the Supreme Court nomination process. Groups mobilize to affect presidential selection and confirmation. The news media become the object of group, White House, and Senate attention but offer their own independent contribution as well. The public weighs in with opinions on the merits of confirmation.

6

Reforming the Process

Clearly, these external players will not go away. For groups or the media or the public to lose interest, the judicial branch would have to be stripped of policy-making power, an unlikely occurrence since it has become a useful branch of last resort for various stripes of issue activists—not to mention the fact that the Court itself is not inclined to divest itself of political power.

The introduction of these forces has created a process divergent from that outlined in the Constitution. It produces a hybrid process, where the constitutional requirements that favor elites and exclude the general public collide with the current version of the process, where external forces, including the general public, actually help shape the outcome. The formal outline of the process should conform to what the process actually has become.

The judicial selection process was designed under the Constitution as elite-dominated. However, that domination is now challenged by the role of external forces. They perform functions today that were not acknowledged originally in the Constitution. The process statutorily and perhaps even constitutionally should be changed to reflect the reality of external players rather than the false idea of exclusive elite involvement.

Changing our public official selection processes to reflect democratic trends is hardly a new feature of American politics. Both presidential and senatorial selection modes have been reformed to acknowledge democratic trends. These institutions have survived such changes.

The Supreme Court selection process similarly needs restructuring to reflect the permanent roles of these external players. That reform is essential, not only at the confirmation stage but also earlier, during the nominee selection process.

Presidential Nomination

One method of reforming the Supreme Court selection process is by constitutional amendment, such as a mandatory retirement age for justices.[1] But constitutional rewording is not the only method for altering the appointment process. In fact, most of the proposed reforms discussed in this chapter would not need to be achieved through constitutional amendment or statutory change. They could occur from the altered behavior of participants of the process, brought about largely by pressure from the public, the press, and perhaps even groups.

One such change regards the president's approach to nominations as thematic tools. Presidents should avoid articulating public themes for their Supreme Court nominations as they have in recent years. Richard Nixon promised to appoint Southerners and strict constructionists.[2] In 1980, Reagan promised to pick justices who shared his judicial philosophy.[3] Echoing Richard Nixon, George W. Bush stated as his theme that he would appoint only strict constructionists.[4] But future presidents should avoid such a publicly thematic approach.

One reason for such avoidance is pragmatic. The nominee who finally emerges from the selection process will be judged against the previously stated administration objective. If they are found wanting, then they are diminished; they are rightly perceived as less than what the president really wanted. Certainly, neither Ruth Bader Ginsburg nor Stephen Breyer fit the politician motif. There was little evidence that they possessed the "big heart" Clinton wanted. Moreover, Stephen Breyer, although arguably the more political of the two on account of his Senate staff experience, lacked any compelling life story that would conform to the model of broad real-world experience. Despite the White House's hints that the president wanted to appoint two justices who were not from the federal judiciary, that is exactly what Clinton ultimately did.

Another reason for avoiding thematic nominations concerns respect for the Court itself. A public statement that the Court needs a certain type of person there at a given time is damaging to the Court's prestige and role. The politician motif Clinton employed suggested that the Court was weighted heavily toward nonpoliticians and needed a mixture including politicians. The implication that the Court did not need another judge from the federal bench suggested that there were too many there already.

If the president seeks to impose a theme on the selection process, it is best done privately without raising public expectations. Or, at least to address the first concern here, it should be announced after the selection (obviously assuring that the individual corresponds to the theme) rather than before.

The presidential interview process also is in need of reformation. The Clinton administration was egregious in toying with Stephen Breyer in the public spotlight. Such embarrassment need not occur. An administration can conduct successive or even nearly simultaneous presidential interviews (as the Bush administration did with Judges David Souter and Edith Jones).[5] In such a situation, no single candidate receives undue publicity. Or it can handle such interviews privately, as the Reagan administration did with O'Connor and the Clinton administration later did with Ginsburg.

A third option is to forgo interviews altogether. That option is particularly useful when the president is already personally familiar with the nominee, but this option still may be the best in all circumstances. Interviews convey the impression that the president and the justice need to establish a personal rapport. If the president was appointing a cabinet member or staff aide with whom he or she would work over a term in office, such personal rapport may be useful. But presidents and Supreme Court justices have little personal interaction. Personal characteristics the president might assess in an interview are not relevant to a justice's functioning on the Court. Moreover, the abandonment of a personal interview does not place the nominee in the awkward position of explaining to senators what he or she said to the president or what the president may have asked of the nominee. The presidential interview is overrated and should be discarded.

Administrations should avoid undue haste in filling a vacancy. At one extreme, the ink was barely dry on Justice William Brennan's retirement letter when David Souter was tapped to fill his place. On the other hand, prolonged hesitation is unwise. The Clinton administration's vacuum encouraged intense interest group lobbying—both direct and indirect—and placed potential nominees in the uncomfortable position of a long period of uncertainty in the glare of public scrutiny.

The administration should be forced, either by statute or press and public expectation, to name a replacement within a certain period of time, preferably 30 but not more than 60 days. Similarly, the Senate should be expected or required to vote on a nominee during a period no longer than 90 and preferably 60 days. Such a rule would prevent a recurrence of the lengthy Bork confirmation process. From presidential announcement to final Senate vote, the Bork nomination dragged on for a seemingly interminable 115 days.

Senate Confirmation

The Senate's role also could stand significant improvement. One critical reform would be a new approach to confirmation hearings. Senators and nominees go through a high-profile charade during confirmation hearings. Senators pretend to ask questions the nominee will actually answer, while nominees pretend to answer the questions the senators actually ask. One senator charged that the hearings "are now producing evasion."[6]

In reality, the hearing stage has become a ceremony designed for the media, interest groups, public opinion, and even fellow senators. Too many senators do not ask the questions that should be posed; in fact, many do not even ask very many questions at all, instead choosing to use their time as a pulpit preacher rather than as a questioner. Given that senators relish an opportunity to articulate their pet concerns about current policy issues or the role of the judiciary in front of television cameras and a large group of reporters, such behavior is understandable. However, it does little to accomplish the apparent objective of the sessions, which is illuminating the views of the nominee.

The purposes of the public ceremony change, depending on whether the nomination has evoked controversy. In the case of the Bork and Thomas hearings, the primary audience was the external players, even the general public. Most senators, many of whom had committed themselves prior to the hearings, used the sessions to defend or condemn the nominee even before hearing testimony.

Consensual nominations, such as the Ginsburg and Breyer nominations, receive more limited press attention, and the goals shift. The ceremony, then, is designed for interest groups who seek to place the nominee on record on pet issues or at least attract the nominee's attention to their issue of concern. Hearings are also used to impress other senators. Few senators want to use only a fraction of their time and be seen as merely acquiescing to an appointment. In the media age, the opportunity to hold the spotlight is not one lightly thrown away.

The questioning problem occurs with more controversial nominations, when the nominee's opponents use queries to highlight the nominee's weaknesses and proponents of the nominee labor to undo the damage caused by their colleagues on the other side. A spate of criticism about inappropriate questions arose following the Robert Bork confirmation process. Another round of scrutiny of the process occurred after the Thomas hearings. These criticisms have continued in recent years with hearings for lower federal appellate judges. The censure has been directed at questions that attempted to commit the nominee in future cases or seek the nominee's opinions on specific cases already decided.

Some of the questions in the past have been of the nature of an inquisition. Repeatedly, questions with the preface "Have you ever . . ." have been posed to nominees. That should not be the focus of inquiry of such sessions. Such lines of inquiry sound too much like the Army-McCarthy hearings of the 1950s. These questions are not related to the breaking of laws or judicial ethics but to past conversations, discussions, and attitudes. Even in controversial nominations, senators should avoid such questioning.

But the committee's public inquiry role can be just as problematic when the nomination is not very controversial. Particularly if the nomination is less controversial and everyone assumes the nominee will be confirmed, some senators use much of their time to "educate" the nominee on areas of the law of interest to the senator or on perspectives toward the law or certain issues they would like the nominee to share.

For example, in one exchange, addressing the issue of capital punishment, Senator Paul Simon of Illinois urged Judge Breyer to "read Justice Powell's reflections at some point. Justice Powell started off pretty much where you are starting off and decided that his original opinion was wrong."[7] Simon implied that Breyer needed to be educated on capital punishment and, as a result, would become better informed and change his opinion on the issue.

The nominee appears to listen to these instructions. How can they do otherwise without offending senators? Yet, what is the point? It is highly unlikely any of these lectures influence subsequent behavior on the bench.

Sometimes senators seek to sway not only policy stances but also the nominee's approach to the job of justice. Senator Simon encouraged Breyer to "spell out specifically for yourself how you really will keep in touch with reality, the reality that a great many Americans face, that, frankly, you are just not going to see."[8]

Senators diminish their investigative role when they ask meaningless "softball" questions. When a senator already has endorsed the nominee's confirmation, his or her questions are so soft that the nominee occasionally even acknowledges it. Often the questions are unrelated to any specific legal issue and are more appropriate for a beauty pageant. Senator William Cohen of Maine asked Breyer what the ten most important books were in his library. Senator Herbert Kohl of Wisconsin asked what the most important problems in society were.[9]

During their allotted time, many senators are often not articulating their own questions but are merely reading those prepared by staff and/or forwarded by interest groups. Some senators even publicly acknowledge that the questions they ask are not theirs, as Senator Pressler did in the anecdote described earlier. When senators allow their interrogatory role to be captured by interest groups, they seriously diminish the committee's status as an investigative body. They feed the perception that they serve only as conduits for interest groups rather than as thoughtful deliberators of the qualifications of a nominee.

Because others prepare many of the questions, senators do not engage in enough follow-up. They allow the nominee to offer a well-prepared nonreply that avoids answering the question. When nominees use boilerplate answers to reply to the senators' boilerplate questions, we have to wonder about the value of such a process.

If the nominee is widely acknowledged as a stellar individual who belongs on the Court—that is, a consensus nominee—the Senate Judiciary Committee should reduce its hearing time. Even three days of testimony, as was the case with both Ginsburg and Breyer, were unnecessary because of the large volume of softball questions asked by senators.

Hearings should not disintegrate into meaningless encounters designed for interest group satisfaction or public consumption. The Senate Judiciary Committee members must perform their investigative task with greater seriousness. They must restore their legitimate role and be willing to hold interest groups at bay.

The role of senators in the confirmation process also is undermined by the tendency to jump on the bandwagon of early support or opposition to a nominee. Too often senators preface their questions to a nominee with an admission of support. Frequently, senators rush to judgment, usually in support, within hours of a nomination announcement. Although such statements usually are qualified to admit the possibility of new information emerging during the confirmation process, their laudatory tone makes retreat nearly impossible. As a result, the subsequent inquest by the committee is tainted by the senators' position pronouncements long before any questions are asked. Senator Arlen Specter of Pennsylvania has been almost alone in urging senators to delay assessing a nominee's fitness until after the evidence is in.[10]

One reason some senators announce a quick verdict on a nominee is their involvement in the White House selection process. Consulting with the president (especially if the president asks whether support would be given if candidate X is nominated) places the senator in a position of being co-opted by the White House. If the senator expresses a position at that point in time, and the president takes the senator's advice, it is expected that the senator will follow through with the commitment and express early support for the nominee. In such a case, the senator is trading independence in the confirmation process for a role in the selection process.

In those situations, senators should publicly acknowledge that they played a role. That way their subsequent statements of support can be viewed in the light of commitments made to the White House in advance. In fairness to constituents, senators ethically cannot have it both ways. They cannot be insiders in the selection process and then act as independent forces during a confirmation process.

Although advice and consent of the Senate is constitutionally mandated, it has been interpreted over the years primarily as Senate involvement after a presidential decision-making process, not during it. Senators are pleased to be consulted by the president. But, in the future, such senators should consider the cost to their ability to independently assess a nominee's worthiness to sit on the Supreme Court.

The problem is, however, specific to a few senators. Most senators are not consulted by the White House during the selection process. That consultation, if it occurs at all, usually is limited to senior Judiciary Committee members and Senate party leaders. Hence, other senators should be free to bide their time in passing judgment on a nominee.

In the case of opposition, Senator Kennedy announced his immediate opposition to Judge Bork in order to slow down the pace of early endorsements. Although this strategy could have conformed to a more independent and thoughtful deliberation by the Senate, in fact the goal was to create momentum in the opposite direction and to make Bork's rejection appear inevitable. Senators who at least publicly withhold judgment until after the investigative reports are written and the committee hearings occur are fulfilling the consent role more appropriately.

Another problem with committee questioning is its length and repetitiveness. The Senate is a highly individualistic institution. Committees are run similarly. However, that individualism means each senator is allowed to have his or her day in the sun at the expense of the nominee, who must endure several days of redundancy, and at the expense of the public, who become bored by the tedium of repetition. Junior senators often repeat questions posed earlier, or they turn to questions on narrow components of the law relevant to their constituency. Some resort to the beauty contest questions.

The committee would do well to pool questions. There is precedent for this. In the second round of hearings in the Thomas confirmation process, designated questioners used much of the allotted time. Such a process is worth repeating in many confirmations. The responsibility of questioning could be rotated to offer the spotlight across the committee membership.

Another solution is to allow the bulk of questioning to be conducted by the majority and minority counsel rather than by the senators themselves.[11] It is unlikely counsel would view nationally televised question time as an opportunity to enhance their electoral careers as senators do.[12] This tactic could increase the likelihood that appropriate questions were asked, but not repeated incessantly, and that irrelevant questions were discarded. Former Senator Paul Simon recommended professional counsel play a larger role in questioning.[13]

This would limit the length of hearings and reduce the number of frivolous questions.

Senators' practices are not the only ones in need of change; the manner in which nominees answer questions has rendered the exercise of hearings nearly meaningless. Nominees have been discouraged by the White House from articulating personal positions on issues. The tactic stems not so much from judicial ethics as from practicality.

At the White House's urging, nominees take seriously the advice given to Judge Ginsburg by a White House aide mentioned earlier, that she was "more likely to lose votes for what you say than what you don't say." As a result, nominees frequently resort to nonreply answers that give the illusion of a reply but offer no substantive information about the nominee. Some senators become upset when a nominee refuses to answer a question. The key difference is in image, not substance. Senators don't like to be told a witness cannot answer their question. They perceive it as demeaning to their status. But, more important, the result is the same. Committee members know little more about a nominee's views after such an exchange than before.

Nominees have varied in reliance on nonreplies. Appellate nominee Miguel Estrada avoided stating positions on past cases, even suggesting at one point that he had not thought enough about the landmark *Roe v. Wade* case to formulate an opinion about it.[14] Antonin Scalia used the tactic repeatedly, even to the point of failing to comment on whether *Marbury v. Madison* was correctly decided.[15] Robert Bork, on the other hand, broadened the range of acceptable replies by freely discussing his views about past cases, current legal issues, and his overarching legal philosophy.

When nominees have departed from that safe haven of judicial propriety, they have suffered. Robert Bork's willingness to engage the committee in discussions of legal philosophy and defend many of his views on specific legal issues and even specific cases became a model to *avoid* for successive nominees.

Although in some cases the nominee may be honest in expressing uncertainty about opinions on various legal issues, in other cases such ambiguity cannot be an accurate reflection of the nominee's thinking.

For example, judging from their subsequent behavior on the bench, it is highly probable that most of the appointees to the Supreme Court in the last few decades held strong views on policy issues, even during the confirmation process, which helped form their votes once on the bench.

Nominees learn either on their own or from White House or Justice Department advisors that the senators' questions are not opportunities to engage in dialogue on important legal issues. Rather, they represent the interests of groups who are concerned about the issue. Justice Breyer explained how he approached the questioners as representatives: The senator "is asking the question because people whom he's elected to represent or some group thereof, have an interest in finding out what you think about it. Now, treat him as representative of those people."[16]

Because a potentially large audience is watching from outside the committee room, the nominee must address their concerns and do so in a manner that communicates the intended message. According to Breyer, the nominee should explain the answer "in language that a person who is not a lawyer can understand. . . . Remember in your language and remember in your explanation that you're trying to say things in words that will in fact be comprehensible to the people who are watching you because they are reflecting those people."[17] Hence, the language the nominee uses reflects an awareness of the broader audience. It must be comprehensible and nonlegalistic.

Even though nominees cannot be forced to do so, they should be willing to express their personal views on issues. It is not a violation of judicial ethics for nominees to state their personal views on issues, even when those issues may be represented in some form in future cases.

One may question the logic of asking such questions. Supreme Court justices, like others who develop opinions on issues, often change their minds over the course of their careers. Therefore, as a guide for future voting, such admissions are hardly perfect. For example, Harry Blackmun probably would not have stated during confirmation hearings that he would vote to overturn existing abortion laws two years later. It was not because Blackmun would have been lying but because his views were transformed as he faced the issue as a Supreme Court justice.

A nominee who serves on the Court for 10, 20, or even 30 years cannot predict future opinions that far in advance. Ronald Rotunda notes that questions about personal views ignore the fact that "we do not know what the major legal questions will be ten years from now, much less thirty years. Nor do we know what the liberal or conservative answers to those questions will be."[18]

Will the expression of views during confirmation hearings lock a justice into a position of imposing that view on future decisions? No. As an example, prior to her confirmation Justice Sandra Day O'Connor expressed her view that abortion was "something that is repugnant to me. . . ." Yet, Justice O'Connor later became a critical vote in Court decisions to uphold a woman's right to an abortion.[19]

In some cases, the nominee's views on particular legal issues may be in a preformed condition, meaning he or she really has not reached a conclusion. The nominee should state that fact. If that reply did not become too common, it could be accepted as a genuine statement. Clarence Thomas's dodge that he had never "debated" *Roe v. Wade*, meant to imply that he had not discussed it, was treated with the skepticism it deserved.[20] When nominees have established views, they should state them.

Acknowledging one's personal views, however, is not the same as promising a certain behavior once on the Court. Nominees should never imply that they would vote a certain way on future cases. They can, and should, freely acknowledge that their personal views do affect the way they perceive the cases before them, but as one of several factors and not always the prevailing one.

The committee and the nation both benefit from knowing not only the legal qualifications of nominees but also the way they view the world. Protesting that personal views are irrelevant is a false claim. The consistency with which many justices have viewed major cases belies that argument. Various blocs on the Court—conservatives, liberals, and the swing votes—develop precisely because personal views do matter. The Supreme Court has the power to affect people's lives, yet the judicial branch is unelected. In a democracy, the people should have the right to examine candidates for the Court, including their views on issues that will affect the lives of citizens.

Reforming the Process: Constitutional Change

Again, the dramatic difference between the Supreme Court selection process today and that of only a generation ago is the public nature of the process. Players external to the White House, the Senate, and the Court now exercise significant roles. That public nature goes beyond the inclusion of television, although that alone is a critical change. It is also the expectation that has accompanied television. That is the belief that judicial selection is a process that the public not only is but also should be a part of.

This expectation is demonstrated even in the more closed process of presidential decision making. Presidents consider whether the nominee will meet with public favor. Public favor is measured initially by reaction from two actors—the news media and interest groups. But both consider themselves, at least to some extent, representatives of the public at large. Presidents gauge such reaction by trial balloons. White House staff members leak names of candidates under consideration. Sometimes these leaks reflect more the interest of the staff member than the president. Nevertheless, a public vetting process occurs.

Reaction comes from interest group leaders, legal scholars, and newspaper editorial writers. If the candidacy seems serious enough, reporters may begin investigative work on the possible nominee. Groups will begin their own investigations, if they have not already. In the case of prospective nominees such as Bush White House Counsel Alberto Gonzales or appeals court Judge J. Harvie Wilkinson, whose potential candidacies were widely acknowledged during the early years of the George W. Bush presidency, groups had long since acquired relevant information to pass on to media, senators, and their own constituencies in the event of their nominations. In other cases, such as lesser known candidates like David Souter and Anthony Kennedy, groups scramble to research opinions, speeches, and personal records. Such research is translated into extensive reports that become the source material for news stories about the president's short list.

Presidential decision making places heavy emphasis on the image that the White House will construct about the nominee. President Clinton was moved by the life story of Ruth Bader Ginsburg and perceived Ginsburg's background as a positive life story easily conveyed in the White House image-making process, thus facilitating her choice as nominee.

The Case for Electing Justices

Since the selection process has become such an open book and the public already is involved as a player, one possible reform is to formalize that involvement by allowing the public to participate in the selection of justices, as is done in some form in most states.

State electoral systems vary in the form of judicial selection for courts of last resort.[21] In 21 states, the electorate participates in the selection of state Supreme Court justices through either partisan or nonpartisan elections. In an additional 13 states, the justices initially are appointed by the governor, typically on the recommendation of merit commissions. Yet, to maintain office beyond a brief initial period, they must pass periodic votes by the general electorate.

Therefore, in two-thirds of the states, the electorate already participates in judicial selection of supreme courts, and in three-fourths of the states, the electorate elects judges at some level.[22] Most states, then, have long since abandoned the federal model of noninvolvement by the electorate.[23]

Judicial elections are not a new idea at the national level elsewhere. A 2002 survey of Canadians found that two-thirds wanted to elect justices of the Canadian Supreme Court rather than have them appointed, as they are currently. Canadian justices are already subject to term limits in the sense that they must retire by the age of 75, unlike their U.S. counterparts, who hold life terms.[24]

A two-stage selection process for a nonpartisan election could be implemented with the objective of preserving the presidential nominating role, as well as a role for the Senate. Several variations on election plans could work. They range from those most inclusive of the public to others using the public as a last resort for decision making.

Under one plan, the president would nominate a set number of candidates, perhaps three, for the general election ballot. This nominating process would weed out self-starters waging entrepreneurial campaigns for the Supreme Court, much as presidential candidates do today. True, lobbying the president to include certain candidates for nomination would occur, but that happens now.

The Senate would play an advisory role for the public—scrutinizing the records of nominees, holding public hearings, and then, by a majority vote, issuing recommendations for or against election of each of the candidates. In most cases, a minority report also would emerge. The Senate's recommendations would become a guide for voters, who may have little information about the candidates.

Then, the voters would go to the polls in a general election every two years. Along with members of Congress and, at every other election, the president, justices would be elected. The individual with the highest number of votes would be confirmed. The terms of the justices could be staggered to provide for the election of typically one and, in rare cases of unplanned vacancies, at most no more than two justices. (Current justices would retain their life-term appointments, but all new appointments would be subject to this process.)

Another variation would involve the public in a plebiscite on a Supreme Court nominee. The process would evolve just as it does now. The president would offer a nomination, and the Senate would deliberate and vote on the nominee. However, the Senate vote would not be the final vote to achieve confirmation. The nominee also would have to win a popular vote—a plebiscite. If the Senate voted in the negative, the nomination would die at that point. Similarly, if the electorate voted no after the Senate had voted to confirm, the nomination would fail. If the nomination failed, the president would be allowed to make a recess appointment until the next election, when the process would be repeated to fill the remainder of the 18-year term.

Still another more limited public role would require an election if a nominee failed to win more than 60 percent of the Senate vote. A controversial (probably constituency-based) nominee would be subject to election while a consensual nominee would not. This provision would encourage presidents to choose consensual nominees to avoid an election.

Any method involving election would require swifter action on the part of the president and the Senate in the judicial selection process than is required now. Because voters would be required to have sufficient time to study the backgrounds of the individual justices, the Senate could be required to make a decision (or recommendation) no later than 60 days before a scheduled federal election. Similarly, the president, knowing well in advance that a vacancy will occur, could be required to submit a nomination (or more than one) by June 1 of the election year.

Although the idea of voting for a Supreme Court justice may be unsettling to many in the legal community, scholars, and observers of the Court, the practice of electing justices is hardly new at the state level. Again, most states have placed state supreme court justices' names on the ballot for years. Nor would this be a completely alien process at the federal level. Elements of the current process would remain in place, with the new wrinkle of final selection by the electorate. Strict limits would have to be placed on the electoral campaign itself. A level playing field would have to be imposed. Under the first proposal, either judicial candidates would be banned from active campaigning or all candidates would be allotted an equal amount of funding with prohibitions on additional spending by themselves or others. Incentives could be provided to media organizations for providing forums for judicial candidates to present themselves to the public.

Is the Public Competent?

Critics of this proposal will point to the inability of the general public to make such decisions about Supreme Court justices. Indeed, Alexander Hamilton made just that claim in explaining why the Court was not subject to popular election under the Constitution. In Federalist 76, Hamilton argued that the people could not function as electors for the Supreme Court because of lack of time: "The exercise of it by the people at large will be readily admitted to be impracticable; as waiving every other consideration, it would leave them little time to do anything else." Clearly, the framers did not intend the public to play a role in judicial election.

Yet in Federalist 68, Hamilton made the same argument about the public's role in electing the president: "A small number of persons, selected by their fellow-citizens from the general mass, will be most likely to possess the information and discernment requisite to such complicated investigations." Hamilton's concerns reflected those of many of his colleagues in 1787, who felt the people lacked the capability to participate directly in the process of leader selection.

Those days are long behind us. Presidential selection essentially is in the hands of the public. True, the 2000 election proved that the national aggregate of the electorate's will can be overturned by the electoral college. But the principle of the firm tie between the popular vote and the electoral college vote within each state remains intact. Democratization of the selection processes has occurred in other ways as well—popular election of Senators, direct primary elections of party nominees, and adoption of initiatives and referenda. The only real holdout appears to be the judicial selection process.

Admittedly, justices of the U.S. Supreme Court, as members of the highest court in the land, are not quite on a par with state supreme courts. Nevertheless, voters are called on to make decisions about the qualifications of candidates for positions with potential impact on public policy in the respective states and at the federal level. Why not on judicial appointments at the federal level?

One fear is that the public would not be aware enough of nominees. Voters know less about Supreme Court nominees than they do about presidential candidates. But voters now vote on candidates they know little about. Less than half of the public can name their own member of Congress.[25]

However, even though they do not now have a direct role in the process, voters do follow Supreme Court nominations. During the confirmation process for Ruth Bader Ginsburg in 1993, 48 percent of the public said they followed the nomination at least fairly closely.[26] Fifty-seven percent of the public said they had followed the nomination process of William Rehnquist as chief justice in 1986.[27] This level of public interest is about the same as that shown during the course of a midterm election.[28]

Even more important for decision making, voters hold opinions about confirmation. Fifty-two percent of Americans, according to an ABC News/Washington Post survey, believed that the Senate should confirm Stephen Breyer's nomination, while 10 percent said the Senate should not. One year earlier, 67 percent had an opinion about whether Ruth Bader Ginsburg should be confirmed. Moreover, the number holding opinions about Supreme Court nominees may have increased. A Harris Survey in 1968 found that 44 percent said they were not sure whether Justice Fortas was an able justice.[29] In 1986, 57 percent said they had "no real feelings" or didn't know how to describe their feelings about the nomination of William Rehnquist as chief justice; 44 percent had said that about Sandra Day O'Connor in 1981.[30]

It is unlikely that an election would affect voter attitudes about the Court. Even though voters hold opinions about the judicial nominees, there is evidence they do not continue to follow individual justices once on the Court. For example, a Quinnipiac University poll in late February 2003 asked respondents their opinions of Justice Antonin Scalia. Although Scalia had served on the Court for more than 16 years, 62 percent said they had not heard enough about him to have an opinion.[31]

Elections would formalize a public role while limiting the ability of the news media or groups to claim the mantle of public representative and spokesperson. Admittedly, both would still possess major roles in electoral campaigns. The extent of the role would depend on the details of the electoral system.

For example, if national judicial elections were held like presidential elections, the result would be disastrous. Justices would be strongly inclined to forge alliances with political action committees, adopt popular positions, and avoid gainful employment for a year or two before an election to campaign and acquire broad name recognition.

But crucial distinctions could be made that would separate judicial candidates from such temptations. If the states served as models, a selection process could be devised that could maintain both accountability and political independence.

An essential component of this selection change would be nonpartisan elections. A partisan election closely ties a judicial candidate to one of the two major parties. It may force the individual to adopt positions in accordance with the party platform. Hence, it reinforces the wrong image—the justice as a partisan. As part of any judicial election process, term limits would be imposed. Only three states— New Hampshire, New York, and Rhode Island—have followed the U.S. Constitution's model of life tenure for Supreme Court justices. All others include specific limited terms.[32] Term limits would provide an opportunity for turnover on the Court and also regularize the election process instead of calling elections only in the case of vacancies.

Supreme Court elections would be a standard expectation in the American electoral system and not an occasional activity. That frequency might reduce the level of intensity placed on the selection process that exists now because of the life-term nature of the appointment.

However, the terms must be lengthy enough to allow the justice an opportunity to acquire and utilize expertise. A limit of 18 years, for example, would provide such a balance between turnover and expertise. Eighteen years also would be long enough to avoid using the Supreme Court as a stepping-stone to other offices, particularly the presidency. Obviously, there would be no possibility of reelection, thus avoiding any incentive to tailor decisions to curry public favor for another term.

Opponents of this scheme may argue that even an 18-year term does not offer sufficient independence for the justices. But the current system already erodes that independence in a number of ways, and a quasi-electoral system already exists. Unfortunately, the current process benefits interest groups and the media and, while claiming actions under the mandate of the public, excludes the public directly from the decision-making process.

Moreover, direct public election would offer a check on the president's power over the Court. Appointment of political cronies would be a more difficult exercise with the electorate more directly involved in the process. The president's ability to pack the Court with ideologues also would be more problematic. It would assure that the public actually agrees with such actions.

The Senate today does not perform an adequate check on the president's power. The confirmation power was a more aggressive check in the 1800s than it has been in this century.[33] Confirmation then was hardly a given. In the past century, however, confirmation has been highly frequent, and presidents with a majority in the Senate rarely lose confirmation struggles. Since 1900, 80 percent of nominees have been confirmed.[34] Even with split-party control in recent years, the president's choice is usually confirmed. Despite the change in a presumption of confirmation, three of four Supreme Court nominees have been confirmed since 1969.

The Supreme Court no longer can be viewed as an apolitical institution. Rather, its political role must be defined to promote both accountability and independence. Accountability inheres from selection by the electorate. Independence is born of a selection process that results in a Court not clearly tied to any particular group or force in American life, including other branches of government.

The tide of history at the state level has turned toward more direct public involvement in judicial selection. In this century there has been a concerted effort at the state level to avoid the flaws of direct election by mixing merit selection with retention elections. It is worthwhile to consider such change at the federal level.

The Future

The apprehension surrounding the judicial selection process for the Supreme Court revolves around our uncertainty about the institution itself. We refuse to admit that the Court is significant as a political institution. That is why presidents use litmus tests while claiming their nominees are the best qualified on their merits. It explains why most senators vote on ideological grounds but decline to say so. It also explains why the general public maintain an interest in the result yet are unsure of the extent to which their opinions should be important in determining the outcome.

This dilemma has become more acute as the Court has acted increasingly like the political institution its defenders often claim it is not. Interest groups view the Court as a results-oriented body whose decisions can most effectively be shaped by affecting who gets to make them. The effectiveness in using personnel shifts to affect Court policy undermines the view that the Court is apolitical. That effectiveness is demonstrated in the Reagan and Bush administrations' success in tilting the Court away from the liberal social activism of the Warren and Burger years.

President Clinton's first selection process came close to tearing away the veneer of an apolitical process. Interest groups learned that the presidential nomination stage could be manipulated. The administration's receptiveness to external forces' efforts emboldened groups to attempt to achieve their political objectives at the presidential selection stage of the process rather than later.

The choices made by the president and senators have a profound impact on American politics and life. President Clinton expressed this sense of responsibility at a speech to a Boys Nation conference on the day Stephen Breyer was confirmed to the U.S. Supreme Court:

Someone needs to be free to decide what the Constitution requires of the rest of us, without the pressures of day-to-day politics. But that imposes on the President and on the United States Senate a very heavy responsibility to pick someone with the character and wisdom to use that awesome power and that lifetime guarantee in the interest of our Constitution, our values and all the American people, without regard to their race, their income, their background.[35]

Judicial selection matters. That is why so many players now crowd the process to affect the outcome. The question is not why the process has become more open but really why a system dominated by a small set of elites lasted so long.

The current process may be bemoaned as denigrating to the Court, and in its extreme forms, when private video records are examined and emphasis is placed on sexual habits or orientation or youthful activities, that complaint is valid. But personnel selection in a democracy is rarely a pristine process. Selection of other policy makers throughout our nation's history has been fraught with problems. The presidential selection process today is hardly an exercise dominated by a wise philosopher-king.

Judicial selection has become much like other forms of leadership selection in the United States. Moreover, it is impossible to put the genie back in the bottle and return to an apolitical ideal. Therefore, rather than ignore the democratic changes in the selection process or condemn them, the nation should adjust to them by designing a judicial selection process that matches the democratization present in American politics while securing a judicial branch capable of defending its independence.

Appendix

A Note on Methodology

To examine print and broadcast media coverage of recent Supreme Court nominations, a content analysis of news stories was conducted covering the period 1981 to 1994. News stories were drawn from the *New York Times, Time,* and *ABC World News Tonight,* although *ABC World News Tonight* stories were obtained only from 1990 on because they were not available in the Nexus database for the previous period.

The stories were placed in seven categories representing the seven vacancies on the Court during this period. They were not organized by nominee but by vacancy. In the case of the Lewis Powell vacancy in 1987, for example, coverage of the three nominees was combined.

This method captured the presidential selection stage prior to announcement of a nominee. Such a stage was nonexistent in one case (Rehnquist/Scalia) because their nominations were announced at the same time as Burger's retirement. In other cases (such as Bork/ Ginsburg/Kennedy, Souter, and Thomas), the selection stage was brief because the administration chose nominees within days of the announcement of the vacancy. But it was an important and lengthier stage during the O'Connor nomination, which lasted 18 days, and especially for the Ruth Bader Ginsburg nomination, where that stage lasted nearly three months.

Still a third part of the study surveyed abstracts of network television evening news broadcasts of the three major broadcast networks between 1990 and 1994. These abstracts were obtained from the Vanderbilt Television News Archive.

Note that because each data source organizes and categorizes news items differently, the usage of different sources meant that the sample drawn from each source varied slightly, even for the same medium from the same period of time.

Notes

Introduction

1. For example, when asked in a Gallup survey whether President Clinton should appoint a woman or a minority to fill the current vacancy "or don't you think he should pay attention to such matters when choosing a Supreme Court nominee," 70 percent agreed with the latter statement. *The Gallup Poll Monthly*, April 1994, p. 30.
2. Eagle Forum, "America at Critical Crossroads—Massive Grassroots Court Reform Campaign Needed Now," at http://www.eagleforum .org/court_watch/reports/2001/6-27-01/part1.shtml.
3. Jonathan Groner, "Nominees Face Democratic Slowdown," *The Legal Intelligencer*, February 3, 2003, p. 4.
4. See "Judicial Nominees Special Report: Our Courts at Risk," at http:// www.now.org/issues/legislat/nominees/index.html; and People for the American Way at http://www.savethecourt.org.
5. Noelle Straub, "Hatch Presses for Action on Judicial Nominees," *The Hill*, December 4, 2002, p. 16.
6. Ibid.
7. Helen Dewar, "Daschle Urges Bush to Consult on High Court Picks," *Washington Post*, June 18, 2003, p. A2; and "White House Rejects Daschle Request for Meeting on Supreme Court," June 18, 2003, at http:// www.cnn.com, accessed June 18, 2003.
8. Lauren M. Cohen, "Missing in Action: Interest Groups and Federal Judicial Appointments," *Judicature*, November–December 1998, pp. 119–123.

9. See John Maltese, *The Selling of Supreme Court Nominees* (Baltimore: Johns Hopkins University Press, 1995).

10. See, for example, G. Calvin Mackenzie, ed., *Innocent until Nominated: The Breakdown of the Presidential Appointments Process* (Washington: Brookings Institution Press, 2001).

11. U.S. National Archives and Records Administration, http://www.archives.gov/federal_register/electoral_college/2000/laws.html#top.

12. See Kenneth W. Goings, *The NAACP Comes of Age: The Defeat of Judge John J. Parker* (Bloomington: Indiana University Press, 1990); and A. L. Todd, *Justice on Trial* (New York: McGraw-Hill, 1964).

13. Regarding the Robert Bork nomination, see, for example, Ethan Bronner, *Battle for Justice: How the Bork Nomination Shook America* (New York: W. W. Norton, 1989); Patrick McGuigan and Dawn M. Weyrich, *The Ninth Justice: The Fight for Bork* (Washington: Free Congress Research and Education Foundation, 1990); Michael Pertschuk and Wendy Schaetzel, *The People Rising: The Campaign against the Bork Nomination* (New York: Thunder's Mouth Press, 1989). For the Thomas nomination, see Timothy M. Phelps and Helen Winternitz, *Capitol Games: The Inside Story of Clarence Thomas, Anita Hill, and a Supreme Court Nomination* (New York: HarperPerennial, 1993).

14. See Jill Zuckman, "GOP Struggle on Race Issue Grows Harder; Bush Nomination Obscures Outreach," *Chicago Tribune*, January 9, 2003, p. 10; Wayne Washington, "Democrats Call Judicial Picks Disappointing Choices," *Boston Globe*, January 9, 2003, p. A2.

15. Zuckman, "GOP Struggle on Race Issue," p. 1; Washington, "Democrats Call Judicial Picks" p. A2; and "Too Smart for the Senate," *Wall Street Journal*, September 5, 2002, p. A14 (editorial).

16. Neil A. Lewis, "Impasse on Judicial Pick Defies Quick Resolution," *New York Times*, March 30, 2003, p. A16.

17. Sarah A. Binder, "The Senate as a Black Hole? Lessons Learned from the Judicial Appointments Experience," in G. Calvin Mackenzie, ed., *Innocent until Nominated*, 173–195.

18. Ibid.

19. John F. Dickerson and Viveca Novak, "Bush's Supreme Challenge," *Time*, May 26, 2003.

20. William G. Ross, "The Supreme Court Appointment Process," *Albany Law Review* 56 (1994): 1023.

Chapter 1

1. Philippa Strum, *Louis D. Brandeis: Justice for the People* (Cambridge, Mass.: Harvard University Press, 1984), pp. 293–298.

2. Ruth Bader Ginsburg, "Confirming Supreme Court Justices: Thoughts on the Second Opinion Rendered by the Senate," *University of Illinois Law Review* 101 (1988): 112.

3. U.S. Constitution, Article II, section 2.

4. John W. Dean, *The Rehnquist Choice: The Untold Story of the Nixon Appointment That Redefined the Supreme Court* (New York: Touchstone, 2001), p. 39.

5. For a discussion of this development, see Theodore J. Lowi, *The Personal President* (Ithaca, N.Y.: Cornell University Press, 1985).

6. Dan Balz and Richard Morin, "Like Father, Bush Gets Postwar Boost," *Washington Post*, May 2, 2003, p. A26.

7. David A. Yalof, *Pursuit of Justices: Presidential Politics and the Selection of Supreme Court Nominees* (Chicago: University of Chicago Press, 1999), pp. 55–61, 193.

8. Dean, *The Rehnquist Choice*, p. 69.

9. See John Massaro, *Supremely Political: The Role of Ideology and Presidential Management in Unsuccessful Supreme Court Nominations* (Albany: State University of New York Press, 1990).

10. Fred P. Graham, "Dirksen Defends Johnson's Naming Friends to Court," *New York Times*, July 13, 1968, p. 1.

11. See, for example, Laurence H. Tribe, *God Save This Honorable Court* (New York: Random House, 1985); and Paul Simon, *Advice and Consent: Clarence Thomas, Robert Bork, and the Intriguing History of the Supreme Court's Nomination Battles* (Washington: National Press Books, 1992).

12. For example, see "Sharp Questions for Judge Breyer," *New York Times* editorial, July 10, 1994, p. E18; and "Searching for Judge Souter," *New York Times*, July 29, 1990, p. E18.

13. Mark Silverstein, *Judicious Choices: The New Politics of Supreme Court Confirmations* (New York: W. W. Norton, 1994), p. 4.

14. Roy M. Mersky and J. Myron Jacobstein, compilers, *The Supreme Court of the United States: Hearings and Reports on Successful and Unsuccessful Nominations of Supreme Court Justices by the Senate Judiciary Committee, 1916–1972* (Buffalo, N.Y.: William S. Hein, 1975).

15. See Massaro, *Supremely Political.*

16. Joan Biskupic, "Election Still Splits Court: Friction Over Justices' Ruling on Ballot Count in Florida Continues to Cause Hard Feelings, Draw Angry Letters, Even Spark Talk of at Least One Imminent Retirement at High Court," *USA Today,* January 22, 2001, p. 1.

17. John A. Jenkins, "The Partisan: A Talk with Justice Rehnquist, *New York Times Magazine,* March 3, 1985, p. 28.

18. Quoted in Henry J. Abraham, *Justices and Presidents: A Political History of Appointments to the Supreme Court* (New York: Oxford University Press, 1992), pp. 178–179.

19. Ibid., p. 24.

20. For a sample of the criticism from the legal community, see "'What's the Alternative?' A Roundtable on the Confirmation Process," *ABA Journal,* January 1992, p. 41; Stuart Taylor Jr., "What's Really Wrong with the Way We Choose Supreme Court Justices," *American Lawyer,* November 1991, p. 5; Senator Orrin G. Hatch, "The Politics of Picking Judges," *Journal of Law & Politics* 6 (Fall 1989): 36–53.

21. Timothy M. Phelps and Tom Brune, "Supreme Court Seat Shuffle? Judges' Retirements Would Spark First Shift in Decades," *Newsday,* May 18, 2003, p. 23.

22. For the most complete discussion of television news coverage of the U.S. Supreme Court, see Elliot E. Slotnick and Jennifer A. Segal, *Television News and the Supreme Court: All the News That's Fit to Air?* (New York: Cambridge University Press, 1998).

23. Richard Davis, *Decisions and Images: The Supreme Court and the Press* (Englewood Cliffs, N.J.: Prentice Hall, 1994), p. 153.

24. Jacobstein and Mersky, *The Supreme Court,* pp. 13–17.

25. Ibid., p. 99; and Abraham, *Justices, Presidents, and Senators,* pp. 102–103.

26. Abraham, *Justices, Presidents, and Senators,* p. 102.

27. Thomas Karfunkel and Thomas W. Ryley, *The Jewish Seat: Anti-Semitism and the Appointment of Jews to the Supreme Court* (Hicksville, N.Y.: Exposition Press, 1978), pp. 37–58.

28. Ibid., p. 47.

29. Abraham, *Justices, Presidents, and Senators,* pp. 135–137; and Strum, *Louis D. Brandeis,* pp. 296–297.

30. John Anthony Maltese, *The Selling of Supreme Court Nominees* (Baltimore: Johns Hopkins University Press, 1995), pp. 49–51; and Strum, *Louis D. Brandeis*, pp. 294–296.

31. Maltese, *The Selling of Supreme Court Nominees*, pp. 49–51.

32. For an extensive treatment of NAACP involvement in the Parker confirmation process, see Goings, *The NAACP Comes of Age*. See also Jacobstein and Mersky, *The Supreme Court*, pp. 111–122.

33. Abraham, *Justices, Presidents, and Senators*, p. 31.

34. Goings, *The NAACP Comes of Age*, p. 24.

35. Maltese, *The Selling of Supreme Court Nominees*, pp. 59–61.

36. Goings, *The NAACP Comes of Age*, chapter 4.

37. Ibid.

38. Interestingly, Parker was one of those considered for nomination by Franklin Roosevelt in 1937.

39. William E. Leuchtenberg, *The Supreme Court Reborn* (New York: Oxford University Press, 1995), p. 186.

40. Ibid., p. 187.

41. Ibid., pp. 191–199.

42. Beverly B. Cook, "Women as Supreme Court Candidates: Florence Allen to Sandra O'Connor," in Kermit L. Hall, ed., *The Supreme Court in American Society: Equal Justice under Law* (New York: Garland, 2000), p. 25.

43. Dean, *The Rehnquist Choice*, p. 3; and Maltese, *The Selling of Supreme Court Nominees*, p. 87.

44. Maltese, *The Selling of Supreme Court Nominees*, pp. 58–59.

45. Ibid., pp. 68–69.

46. Ibid., p. 86.

47. Speech by Senator Joseph Biden on reform of the confirmation process, *Congressional Record*, June 25, 1992, vol. 138, no. 93, p. S8861.

48. See Tony Mauro, "Lloyd's of London Haunts Breyer's High-Court Debut; Does Slew of Cert Recusals Signal a Hobbled Justice," *Legal Times*, October 10, 1994, p. 1; Kathleen Kerr, "Senate Report Rips Foley Sq. Courthouse," *Newsday*, December 14, 1994, p. A4; and Jack Anderson (syndicated column), "Report Slams Breyer's Role in Courthouse Project," (Springfield, Ill.) *State Journal-Register*, December 16, 1994, p. 10.

49. Examples of candidates who withdrew from consideration include New York Governor Mario Cuomo, Senator George Mitchell of Maine, and Secretary of Education Richard Riley.

50. Ronald D. Rotunda, "The Confirmation Process for Supreme Court Justices in the Modern Era," *Emory Law Journal* 37 (Summer 1988): 586.

51. Speech by Senator Joseph Biden on reform of the confirmation process.

52. David P. Bryden, "How to Select a Supreme Court Justice," *American Scholar*, Spring 1988, p. 201.

53. See Norman Viera and Leonard E. Gross, "The Appointments Clause: Judge Bork and the Role of Ideology in Judicial Confirmations," *Journal of Legal History* 11 (December 1990): 311–392.

54. Speech to public administration groups, October 24, 1991, Washington, D.C. Excerpted in *Clarence Thomas: Confronting the Future* (Washington, D.C.: Regnery Gateway, 1992), p. 30.

55. Bruce Fein, "Commentary: A Circumscribed Senate Confirmation Role," *Harvard Law Review* 102 (January 1989): 687.

56. See, for example, Gary J. Simson, "Taking the Court Seriously: A Proposed Approach to Senate Confirmation of Supreme Court Nominees," *Constitutional Commentary* 7 (Summer 1990): 283–324.

57. Stephen Carter, "The Confirmation Mess," *Harvard Law Review* 101 (April 1988): 1185–1201.

58. Nina Totenberg, "The Confirmation Process and the Public: To Know or Not to Know," *Harvard Law Review* (April 1988): 1213–1229.

59. Bruce A. Ackerman, "Transformative Appointments," *Harvard Law Review* 102 (April 1988): 1164–1184.

60. See, for example, Michael J. Gerhardt, "Divided Justice: A Commentary on the Nomination and Confirmation of Justice Thomas," *George Washington Law Review* 60 (1992): 969; and David A. Strauss and Cass R. Sunstein, "The Senate, the Constitution, and the Confirmation Process," *Yale Law Journal* 101 (1992): 1491.

61. See Gary J. Simson, "Thomas's Supreme Unfitness—A Letter to the Senate on Advice and Consent," *Cornell Law Review* 78 (May 1993): 619–663. See David M. O'Brien, *Judicial Roulette: Report of the Twentieth Century Fund Task Force on Judicial Selection* (Washington, D.C.: Brookings Institution, 1988).

62. See Simon, *Advice and Consent*.

63. Barbara Sinclair, "Senate Process, Congressional Politics, and the Thomas Nomination," *PS*, September 1992, pp. 477–480.
64. Ross, "The Supreme Court Appointment Process," 1011–1012.

Chapter 2

1. James Haw, *John & Edward Rutledge of South Carolina* (Athens: University of Georgia Press, 1997), pp. 245–256.
2. See ibid.; and J. Myron Jacobstein and Roy M. Mersky, *The Rejected: Sketches of the 26 Men Nominated for the Supreme Court but Not Confirmed by the Senate* (Milpatas, Calif.: Toucan Valley Publications, 1993), pp. 7–10.
3. Jacobstein and Mersky, *The Rejected*, pp. 33–41.
4. Dean, *The Rehnquist Choice*, p. 47.
5. Abraham, *Justices, Presidents, and Senators*, p. 11.
6. Cook, "Women as Supreme Court Candidates," pp. 23–28.
7. Dean, *The Rehnquist Choice*, pp. 221–240.
8. Jacobstein and Mersky, *The Rejected*, pp. 69–74.
9. Dean, *The Rehnquist Choice*, p. 18.
10. Abraham, *Justices, Presidents, and Senators*, p. 11.
11. Joan Biskupic, "A Kinder, Gentler Confirmation Process," *Washington Post National Weekly Edition*, August 1–7, 1994, p. 15.
12. For discussion of the first stage, presidential selection, see Byron J. Moraski and Charles R. Shipan, "The Politics of Supreme Court Nomination: A Theory of Institutional Constraints and Choices," *American Journal of Political Science* 43 (October 1999): 1069–1095; Yalof, *Pursuit of Justices*; Abraham, *Justices, Presidents, and Senators*; Maltese, *The Selling of Supreme Court Nominees*; George L. Watson and John A. Stookey, *Shaping America: The Politics of Supreme Court Appointments* (New York: HarperCollins, 1995); and Massaro, *Supremely Political*. For a discussion of the process as constituting three stages, see Martin Shapiro, "Interest Groups and Supreme Court Appointments," *Northwestern University Law Review* 84 (Spring–Summer 1990): 936.
13. See, for example, Shapiro, "Interest Groups"; William G. Ross, "Participation by the Public in the Federal Judicial Selection Process," *Vander-*

bilt Law Review 43 (January 1990): 1–84; and Judith Lichtman, "Public Interest Groups and the Bork Nomination," *Northwestern University Law Review* 84 (Spring–Summer 1990): 978–979.

14. "Remarks Announcing the Intention to Nominate Sandra Day O'Connor to Be an Associate Justice of the Supreme Court of the United States July 7, 1981," The Public Papers of President Ronald Reagan, The Ronald Reagan Library, at http://www.reagan.utexas.edu/resource/speeches/rrpubpap.asp.

15. "Excerpts from News Conference Announcing Court Nominee," *New York Times*, July 2, 1991, p. A14.

16. Henry J. Abraham, *Justices and Presidents*, p. 73.

17. Reagan, "Remarks Announcing the Intention."

18. Abraham, *Justices and Presidents*, pp. 71–79.

19. Dean, *The Rehnquist Choice*, p. 88.

20. Abraham, *Justices, Presidents, and Senators*, p. 3.

21. The exception was Lewis Powell, a conservative Democrat nominated by Richard Nixon in 1972. Powell became a swing vote on the Court and served until 1987.

22. Yalof, *Pursuit of Justices*, p. 171.

23. For a discussion of presidential reaction to the decisions of their own nominees, see David M. O'Brien, *Storm Center: The Supreme Court in American Politics* (New York: W. W. Norton, 1993), pp. 121–125.

24. Quoted in Abraham, *Justices and Presidents*, p. 70.

25. For a discussion of these criteria, see Abraham, *Justices, Presidents, and Senators*, pp. 2–3.

26. Quoted in Abraham, *Justices and Presidents*, p. 270.

27. Abraham, *Justices, Presidents, and Senators*, pp. 5–6.

28. For a discussion of the ABA's process for grading nominees, see Ross, "Participation by the Public in the Federal Judicial Selection Process"; and Joan M. Hall, "The Role of the ABA Standing Committee on the Federal Judiciary," *Northwestern University Law Review* 84 (1990): 980–981.

29. Dean, *The Rehnquist Choice*, pp. 160–161; and Watson and Stookey, *Sahping America*, pp. 83–85.

30. Letter to the American Bar Association from White House Counsel Alberto Gonzales. Quoted in Robert S. Greenberger, "ABA Loses Major Role in Judge Screening," *Wall Street Journal*, March 23, 2001, p. B8.

31. Greenberger, "ABA Loses Major Role." For a discussion of bias in the ABA's role in judicial nominee evaluation, see James Lindgren, "Examining the American Bar Association's Ratings of Nominees to the U.S. Courts of Appeals for Political Bias, 1989–2000," *Journal of Law & Politics* 17 (Winter 2001): 1–39.

32. Dean, *The Rehnquist Choice*, p. 89.

33. For a brief discussion of this controversy, see Ross, "Participation by the Public in the Federal Judicial Selection Process," pp. 35–41.

34. Linda Greenhouse, "Legal Establishment Divided over Bork Nomination," *New York Times*, September 26, 1987, p. 33.

35. Abraham, *Justices, Presidents, and Senators*, pp. 4, 181.

36. Abraham, *Justices and Presidents*, pp. 72–75.

37. Ronald D. Rotunda, "Innovations Disguised as Traditions: A Historical Review of the Supreme Court Nominations Process," *University of Illinois Law Review* (1995): 123–131.

38. Leuchtenberg, *The Supreme Court Reborn*, pp. 183.

39. For a discussion of the Jewish seat, see Karfunkel and Ryley, *The Jewish Seat*.

40. Eisenhower subsequently appointed William Brennan. Yalof, *Pursuit of Justices*, pp. 55–61.

41. Nelson W. Polsby and Aaron Wildavsky, *Presidential Elections*, 8th ed. (New York: Free Press, 1991), p. 335.

42. Yalof, *Pursuit of Justices*, p. 201.

43. "Diversity on the Supreme Court," *New York Times*, June 9, 1993, p. A20.

44. Tribe, *God Save This Honorable Court*, p. 106.

45. Stuart Taylor Jr., "Politics of the Bench; Carter and Reagan Seek Gains from Prospective Judiciary," *New York Times*, October 28, 1980, p. A27.

46. Dean, *The Rehnquist Choice*, p. 53.

47. Abraham, *Justices and Presidents*, pp. 328–329.

48. Cook, "Women as Supreme Court Candidates," p. 26.

49. Phelps and Winternitz, *Capitol Games*, pp. 137–139, 396; and Steven V. Roberts, "Battling over a Native Son," *U.S. News & World Report*, September 16, 1991, p. 33.

50. "Operation Supreme Court Freedom" letter from Pat Robertson, chairman of the Christian Broadcasting Network, July 15, 2003, at http://cbn.org/special/supremecourt/pledgetopray.asp.

51. For a brief history of the Chase impeachment, see George Lee Haskins and Herbert A. Johnson, *History of the Supreme Court of the United States*, vol. 2 (New York: Macmillan, 1981), pp. 205–245.

52. Dean, *The Rehnquist Choice*, pp. 24–26.

53. Frank Brown Latham, *FDR and the Supreme Court Fight, 1937* (New York: F. Watts, 1972).

54. Dean, *The Rehnquist Choice*, p. 5.

55. Ibid., pp. 5–10.

56. Abraham, *Justices and Presidents*, pp. 249, 283–285.

57. Leuchtenberg, *The Supreme Court Reborn*, pp. 180–181.

58. Yalof, *Pursuit of Justices*, pp. 44–51.

59. Ibid., pp. 156–160.

60. Abraham, *Justices and Presidents*, p. 327.

61. See Yalof, *Pursuit of Justices*, pp. 191–192.

62. Ruth Marcus, "President Asks Wider Court Hunt," *Washington Post*, May 6, 1993, p. A1.

63. Dean, *The Rehnquist Choice*, pp. 46–47.

64. Leuchtenberg, *The Supreme Court Reborn*, pp. 183–184.

65. See Dean, *The Rehnquist Choice*. Based on tapes of Nixon's meetings, the book demonstrates that Mitchell was a frequent participant in Nixon's discussion about Court appointments while Dean was only an occasional one.

66. Ibid., pp. 144–145.

67. For the development of this argument, see Yalof, *Pursuit of Justices*.

68. Ruth Marcus, "Judge Breyer May See Clinton Today," *Washington Post*, June 11, 1993, p. A6.

69. Abraham, *Justices, Presidents, and Senators*, pp. 305–306, 311.

70. "Schumer Sends Bush Suggestions for Supreme Court," June 10, 2003, at http://www.cnn.com/2003/ALLPOLITICS/06/10/schumer.judges.ap/index.html, accessed on June 10, 2003.

71. Yalof, *Pursuit of Justices*, p. 159.

72. Ibid., p. 164.

73. Robin Toner and Neil A. Lewis, "Lobbying Starts as Groups Foresee Supreme Court Vacancy," *New York Times*, June 8, 2003, p. A1.

74. Leuchtenberg, *The Supreme Court Reborn*, p. 183.

75. Abraham, *Justices and Presidents*, pp. 20–21.

76. Ibid., p. 204.

77. Ibid., pp. 186–190. One scholar contends Taft's influence was greater in excluding consideration of certain individuals he opposed rather than in successfully recommending those he favored. See David Michael Stewart, "Supreme Court Appointments during the Harding and Coolidge Administrations: Influence, Critics, and Voting," unpublished Ph.D. dissertation, Wayne State University, 1974.

78. Abraham, *Justices and Presidents*, pp. 8, 19, 244; and Yalof, *Pursuit of Justices*, p. 151.

79. Dean, *The Rehnquist Choice*, pp. 104, 137–138, 179–180.

80. See Stuart A. Taylor Jr., "Justice Stevens, in Unusual Move, Praises Bork as Nominee to Court," *New York Times*, August 1, 1987, p. 1; CBS Evening News Broadcast, September 22, 1987 (the justice was Byron White); and "Marshall Says He Never Heard of Bush's Nominee," *New York Times*, July 27, 1990, p. A12.

81. Abraham, *Justices, Presidents, and Senators*, p. 304.

82. Dean, *The Rehnquist Choice*, p. 36.

83. See Moraski and Shipan, "The Politics of Supreme Court Nominations," and John Massaro, *Supremely Political*.

84. Dean, *The Rehnquist Choice*, p. 108.

85. Ibid., p. 56.

86. John Anthony Maltese, "Speaking Out: The Role of Presidential Rhetoric in the Modern Supreme Court Confirmation Process," *Presidential Studies Quarterly* 25 (Summer 1995): 447–455.

87. Ibid.

88. Maltese, *The Selling of Supreme Court Nominees*, pp. 114–115.

89. Bronner, *Battle for Justice*, pp. 307–327, 334–336.

90. Phelps and Winternitz, *Capitol Games*, p. 412.

91. Rotunda, "Innovations Disguised as Traditions."

92. Abraham, *Justices and Presidents*, p. 222.

93. Robert F. Nagel, "Advice, Consent, and Influence," *Northwestern University Law Review* 84 (Spring–Summer 1990): 859.

94. Paul Simon, *Advice and Consent*, pp. 38–39.

95. Ibid., p. 49.

96. Abraham, *Justices and Presidents*, pp. 27–28.

97. Jeffrey Segal, "Senate Confirmation of Supreme Court Justices: Partisan and Institutional Politics," *Journal of Politics* 49 (November 1987): 1014.

98. Abraham, *Justices, Presidents, and Senators*, p. 329.

99. See, for example, Cecil V. Crabb and Pat M. Holt, *Invitation to Struggle*, 3rd ed. (Washington: CQ Press, 1989); Anthony King, ed., *Both Ends of the Avenue* (Washington: AEI, 1983); and David M. Abshire and Ralph D. Nurnberger, eds., *The Growing Power of Congress* (Beverly Hills, Calif.: Sage, 1981).

100. This has been true even when the president's party controls the Senate. Recent examples from the Clinton presidency include Zoe Baird and Kimba Wood, nominees for attorney general, and Lani Guinier, nominee for associate attorney general for civil rights.

101. Jeffrey A. Segal and Harold J. Spaeth, "If a Supreme Court Vacancy Occurs, Will the Senate Confirm a Reagan Nominee," *Judicature*, December–January 1986, pp. 186–190.

102. The four were Clement Haynsworth (1969), G. Harrold Carswell (1970), Robert Bork, and Douglas Ginsburg (both in 1987). The other two were Abe Fortas and Homer Thornberry (both in 1968).

103. Joel B. Grossman and Stephen L. Wasby, "The Senate and Supreme Court Nominations: Some Reflections," *Duke Law Journal* 21 (1972), p. 560.

104. See Tribe, *God Save This Honorable Court*; and Robert F. Nagel, "Advice, Consent, and Influence."

105. Grover Rees III, "Questions for Supreme Court Nominees at Confirmation Hearings," *Georgia Law Review* 17 (Summer 1983): 913–967.

106. See Forrest Black, "The Role of the United States Senate in Passing on the Nominations to Membership in the Supreme Court of the United States," *Kentucky Law Journal* 19 (1930–1931): 226–238.

107. Nagel, "Advice, Consent, and Influence," p. 859.

108. See Jeffrey A. Segal, Albert D. Cover, and Charles M. Cameron, "The Role of Ideology in Senate Confirmation of Supreme Court Justices," *Kentucky Law Journal* 77 (1988–1989): 485–508; and John D. Felice and Herbert F. Weissberg, "The Changing Importance of Ideology, Party, and Region in Confirmation of Supreme Court Nominees 1953–1988," *Kentucky Law Journal* 7 (1988–1989): 509–530.

109. Segal and Spaeth, "If a Supreme Court Vacancy Occurs"; and Segal, "Senate Confirmation of Supreme Court Justices," pp. 998–1015.

110. Michael A. Kahn, "The Appointment of a Supreme Court Justice: A Political Process from Beginning to End," *Presidential Studies Quarterly* 25 (April 2001): 25–41.

111. Richard Davis, "The Ginsburg Nomination and the Press," *Harvard International Journal of Press/Politics* 1 (Spring 1996): 78–99.

112. Abraham, *Justices and Presidents*, p. 242.

113. Leuchtenberg, *The Supreme Court Reborn*, p. 184.

114. Segal and Spaeth, "If a Supreme Court Vacancy Occurs," pp. 186–190.

115. Abraham, *Justices and Presidents*, pp. 245–247.

Chapter 3

1. R. H. Bork Jr., "The Media, Special Interests, and the Bork Nomination," in McGuigan and Weyrich, *The Ninth Justice*, p. 246.

2. Suzanne Garment, "The War against Robert Bork," *Commentary*, January 1988, p. 19.

3. Pertschuk and Schaetzel, *The People Rising*, p. 4.

4. Gregory A. Caldiera, "Commentary on Senate Confirmation of Supreme Court Justices: The Roles of Organized and Unorganized Interests," *Kentucky Law Journal* 77 (1988–1989): 538.

5. See E. E. Schattschneider, *The Semisovereign People* (Hinsdale, Ill.: Dryden, 1975).

6. See Morris P. Fiorina, *Divided Government* (New York: Macmillan, 1992), chapter 2.

7. Woodrow Wilson, *Congressional Government* (Cleveland, Ohio: World Publishing, 1965).

8. *Constitutional Government of the United States* (New York: Columbia University Press, 1908).

9. Simon, *Advice and Consent*, pp. 311–312.

10. For a sample of this criticism, see Donald L. Horowitz, *The Courts and Social Policy* (Washington, D.C.: Brookings Institution, 1977); Robert H. Birkby, *The Court and Public Policy* (Washington, D.C.: CQ Press, 1983); and Thomas Sowell, *Judicial Activism Reconsidered* (Stanford, Calif.: Hoover Institution, 1989).

11. Mark Silverstein, *Judicious Choices: The New Politics of Supreme Court Confirmations* (New York: W. W. Norton, 1994), pp. 71–72.

12. David E. Rosenbaum, "Emotional Issues Are the 1988 Battleground," *New York Times*, November 4, 1988, p. A1.

13. Ross, "The Supreme Court Appointment Process," p. 1021.

14. Silverstein, *Judicious Choices*, p. 71.

15. Tribe, *God Save This Honorable Court*, p. 93.

16. Simon, *Advice and Consent*, pp. 314–317.

17. "Now, the Clinton Court," *U.S. News & World Report*, March 29, 1993, p. 20.

18. *Planned Parenthood of Southeastern Pennsylvania, et al. v. Casey*, 114 S. Ct. 909 (1992).

19. Ibid.

20. Kim Cobb, "A Liberal Gain for the High Court; Not Enough Senate Votes to Reject Almost Any Clinton Pick," *Houston Chronicle*, March 21, 1993, p. A20.

21. For a discussion of the evolution of this electoral system, see Richard P. McCormick, *The Second American Party System* (New York: W. W. Norton, 1966). For a specific treatment of the evolution in the press, see Richard Rubin, *Press, Party, and Presidency* (New York: W. W. Norton, 1981).

22. For a discussion of press coverage of the policy-making process, see Richard Davis, *The Press and American Politics: The New Mediator*, 2nd ed. (Upper Saddle River, N.J.: Prentice-Hall, 1996), pp. 297–309.

23. For a discussion of the role of news values in the news reporting process, see Doris A. Graber, *Mass Media and American Politics*, 4th ed. (Washington: CQ Press, 1993), pp. 116–120.

24. "National Survey Shows C-SPAN Audience Nearly Doubled in 1988 as It Grew Broader, Younger, More Diverse," C-SPAN press release, January 9, 1989.

25. For a narrative on television in the House of Representatives, see Ronald Garay, *Congressional Television* (Westport, Conn.: Greenwood, 1984).

26. See Stephen Hess, *The Ultimate Insiders: U.S. Senators in the National Media* (Washington: Brookings Institution, 1986), pp. 31–35.

27. Quoted in Richard Benedetto and Tony Mauro, "N.Y.'s Cuomo Bows Out of High Court Contention," *USA Today*, April 8, 1993, p. 2A.

28. "Symington Fields Call from Clinton Regarding Babbitt," *Phoenix Gazette*, June 11, 1993, p. B1.

29. Robert Woodward, *The Agenda* (New York: Simon and Schuster, 1994), p. 86.

30. *Webster v. Reproductive Health Services* 492 U.S. 490 (1989).

31. See, for example, the Court's struggle with affirmative action policies in opinions in cases such as *Regents of the University of California v. Bakke* 438 U.S. 265 (1978), *Firefighters Local Union No. 1784 v. Stotts* 467 U.S. 561 (1984), and *Metro Broadcasting, Inc. v. FCC* 490 U.S. 755 (1990).

32. See Susan Hedman, "Friends of the Earth and Friends of the Court: Assessing the Impact of Interest Group Amici Curiae in Environmental Cases Decided by the Supreme Court," *Virginia Environmental Law Journal* 10 (Spring 1991): 187–212.

33. See, for example, Karen O'Connor, *Women's Organizations' Use of the Courts* (Lexington, Md.: Lexington, 1980); Karen O'Connor and Lee Epstein, *Public Interest Law Groups: Institutional Profiles* (New York: Greenwood, 1989); and Lee Epstein, "Interest Group Litigation during the Rehnquist Court Era," *Journal of Law and Politics* 9 (Summer 1993): 639–717.

34. See Pertschuk and Schaetzel, *The People Rising;* and Phelps and Winternitz, *Capitol Games.*

35. Garment, "The War against Robert H. Bork."

36. For samples, see Angie Cannon, "The Supremes' Future: The Next President Will Make Dramatic Changes on the High Court," *U.S. News & World Report,* May 15, 2000, p. 18; Charles Lane and Amy Goldstein, "At High Court, a Retirement Watch; Rehnquist, O'Connor Top List of Possibilities as Speculation on Replacement Grows, *Washington Post,* June 17, 2001, p. A4; Bob Egelko, "GOP Win Puts Focus on Supreme Court," *San Francisco Chronicle,* November 7, 2002, p. A20; and David G. Savage, "Bush Ally Is Top Contender for Nomination for Supreme Court, *Los Angeles Times,* December 30, 2002, p. 1.

37. "Thomas Takes TV's Center Stage," *Broadcasting,* October 21, 1991, p. 24.

38. Ibid.

39. CBS/*New York Times* survey, October 13, 1991.

40. See Richard Davis, *The Press and American Politics: The New Mediator,* 3rd ed. (Upper Saddle River, N.J.: Prentice Hall, 2001), pp. 143–146.

41. Pertschuk and Schaetzel, *The People Rising,* p. 41.

42. See Davis, *The Press and American Politics: The New Mediator,* 3rd ed.

43. "Thomas Takes TV's Center Stage," p. 24.

44. Garment, "The War against Robert H. Bork," p. 23.

45. Joe Flint, "Totenberg Just Says No to Senate," *Broadcasting*, March 2, 1992, p. 31–32.

Chapter 4

1. Barbara A. Perry, *A "Representative" Supreme Court? The Impact of Race, Religion, and Gender on Appointments* (New York: Greenwood, 1991), p. 131.
2. Douglas E. Kneeland, "The Republican Defends Stance on Equal Rights and War Accusations; Attention Shifts to Women," *New York Times*, October 15, 1980, p. A1.
3. Thomas L. Jipping, "Will Clinton Let Liberals Use Judicial Litmus Test?" *National Law Journal*, December 21, 1992, p. 1.
4. Yalof, *Pursuit of Justices*, p. 193.
5. Timothy M. Phelps and Tom Brune, "Supreme Court Seat Shuffle? Judges' Retirements Would Spark First Shift in Decades," *Newsday*, May 18, 2003, p. 23.
6. Yalof, *Pursuit of Justices*, p. 204.
7. Interview with the Tom Jipping, July 1, 1993.
8. Nina Totenberg, "The Confirmation Process and the Public," p. 1216.
9. Caldeira and Wright, "Lobbying for Justice: Organized Interests, Supreme Court Nominations, and the United States Senate," *American Journal of Political Science* 42 (April 1998): 499–523.
10. Linda Greenhouse, "The Ginsburg Hearings: An Absence of Suspense Is Welcomed," *New York Times*, July 25, 1993, section 4, p. 3.
11. *Nomination of Ruth Bader Ginsburg to Be Associate Justice of the Supreme Court of the United States*, Hearings before the Committee on the Judiciary, United States Senate, One Hundred Third Congress, July 20–23, 1993, pp. 30–31; and *Nomination of Stephen G. Breyer to Be Associate Justice of the Supreme Court of the United States*, Hearings before the Committee on the Judiciary, United States Senate, One Hundred Third Congress, July 12–15, 1994.
12. *Nomination of Ruth Bader Ginsburg to Be Associate Justice of the Supreme Court of the United States*, pp. 131–132.
13. Gwen Ifill, "The Baird Appointment: In Trouble from the Start, Then a Firestorm," *New York Times*, January 23, 1993, p. 8; and Robert D.

McFadden, "The White House and Judge's Allies Clash over Hiring; Contradictory Accounts," *New York Times*, February 7, 1993, p. 1.

14. For a discussion of the timing of retirements, see Artemus Ward, *Deciding to Leave: The Politics of Retirement from the United States Supreme Court* (Albany: State University of New York Press, 2003).

15. Edward C. Burks, "Arizona Judge, a Woman, Is High Court Contender," *New York Times*, July 2, 1981, p. A17.

16. Dean, *The Rehnquist Choice*, p. 23.

17. Ibid., p. 179.

18. Jerry Seper, "Bet on Controversy; Babbitt Nomination to Court Could Revive Talk of Vegas, Mob," *Washington Times*, June 8, 1993, p. A1; Jerry Seper, "Casinos Checked Out Babbitt; His Denials of Gambling Don't Fit Record," *Washington Times*, June 9, 1993, p. A1; and Jerry Seper and Paul Bedard, "Babbitt Still on Court List," *Washington Times*, June 10, 1993, p. A1.

19. Press Briefing by Dee Dee Myers, The White House, Office of the Press Secretary, June 9, 1993.

20. *Newsweek*, June 28, 1993, p. 4.

21. Interview with Justice Ruth Bader Ginsburg, September 17, 1993.

22. Ibid.

23. *Nomination of Stephen G. Breyer to Be Associate Justice of the Supreme Court of the United States*, p. 149.

24. Ibid., pp. 142, 247.

25. Ibid., pp. 468–470.

26. Caldiera, "Commentary on Senate Confirmation of Supreme Court Justice."

27. Kathleen Frankovic and Joyce Gelb, "Public Opinion and the Thomas Nomination," *PS*, September 1992, pp. 481–484.

28. David W. Moore and Lydia Saad, "Public Supports Clinton's Supreme Court Nominee," *The Gallup Poll Monthly*, June 1993, p. 19–20; and ABC News/*Washington Post* survey, June 5, 1994.

29. Gallup Survey, September 2, 1987; Gallup Survey, September 14, 1987.

30. Surveys of opinion toward Ginsburg and Breyer are presented later, but, for a sample of surveys concerning Souter, see Yankelovich Clancy Shulman survey, July 1990; and Thomas A. Fogarty, "Iowans Back Judge Souter for High Court," *Des Moines Register*, September 25, 1990.

31. Times Mirror Center for the People & the Press, Times Mirror News Interest Index, July 18, 1991.

32. See *Los Angeles Times* telephone survey, October 15, 1991; and ABC News telephone survey, October 16, 1991.

33. Elizabeth Kolbert, "The Thomas Nomination; Most in National Survey Say Judge Is the More Believable," *New York Times*, October 15, 1991, p. A1.

34. Times Mirror Center for the People & the Press, Times Mirror News Interest Index, August 5, 1993.

35. Ibid.

36. Frankovic and Gelb, "Public Opinion."

37. Watson and Stookey, *Shaping America*, pp. 118–122.

38. Quoted in Abraham, *Justices, Presidents, and Senators*, p. 292.

39. Watson and Stookey, *Shaping America*, p. 86.

40. Ibid., p. 87.

Chapter 5

1. "Remarks by the President and Judge Ruth Bader Ginsburg in Press Availability," The White House, Office of the Press Secretary, August 3, 1993.

2. Dean, *The Rehnquist Choice*, p. 158.

3. Ibid., p. 187.

4. Ibid., p. 157.

5. See, for example, Elizabeth Kolbert, "The Thomas Nomination."

6. For a discussion of the use of political symbols, see Murray Edelman, *The Symbolic Uses of Politics* (Urbana: University of Illinois Press, 1985).

7. *Time*, September 21, 1987.

8. One exception in the second half of this century was Earl Warren, who had served as governor of California and Republican vice presidential nominee in 1948.

9. One notable exception was Robert Bork, who had been U.S. solicitor general during the Nixon administration and gained public notice for firing Archibald Cox, Watergate special prosecutor, at the behest of the president, in the midst of the Watergate investigation. Both the attor-

ney general and the deputy attorney general refused to fire Cox and either resigned or was fired. Bork followed the president's order.

10. "Press Briefing by White House Counsel Lloyd Cutler and Deputy Counsel Joel Klein," The White House, Office of the Press Secretary, May 13, 1994.

11. "Excerpts from News Conference," p. A14.

12. "President's News Conference on Resignation of Chief Justice," *New York Times*, June 18, 1986, p. A30.

13. Steven R. Weisman, "Reagan Nominating Woman, an Arizona Appeals Judge, to Serve on Supreme Court," *New York Times*, July 8, 1981, p. A1.

14. David G. Savage, "Clinton Aides Still Adding Names to Supreme Court List," *Los Angeles Times*, May 1, 1993, p. A5.

15. Watson and Stookey, *Shaping America*, pp. 115, 117.

16. Quoted in Abraham, *Justices, Presidents, and Senators*, pp. 297–298.

17. Dale Russakoff, "Hunting for Souter's 'Smoking Gun,'" *Washington Post*, July 26, 1990, p. A25.

18. Abraham, *Justices, Presidents, and Senators*, p. 305.

19. Watson and Stookey, *Shaping America*, p. 117.

20. Alliance for Justice, "Report on the Nomination of Judge Ruth Bader Ginsburg to the United States Supreme Court," unpublished document, p. 2.

21. *Nomination of Stephen G. Breyer to Be Associate Justice of the Supreme Court of the United States*, p. 384.

22. Interview with Carl Cannon, *Baltimore Sun* White House correspondent, June 17, 1993.

23. Background interview, August 5, 1993.

24. Ross, "The Supreme Court Appointment Process," pp. 1015–1016.

25. Dewar, "Daschle Urges Bush," p. A2.

26. Watson and Stookey, *Shaping America*, pp. 112–117.

27. Ibid., pp. 117–118.

28. "From Obscure to Unknown," *New York Times*, January 21, 1970, p. 46.

29. Fred P. Graham, "Johnson and the Court; Two Appointments That Don't Please Everybody," *New York Times*, June 30, 1968, p. E1.

30. "How to Judge Judge Bork," *New York Times*, July 7, 1987, p. A26.

31. Interview with Tom Jipping, July 1, 1993.

32. Abraham, *Justices, Presidents, and Senators*, p. 294.

33. Bader Ginsburg, "Confirming Supreme Court Justices," 117.

34. For examples, see Troy Segal, "Getting Serious about Sexual Harassment," *Business Week*, November 9, 1992, p. 78; and Steven V. Roberts, "Will 1992 Be the Year of the Woman," *U.S. News & World Report*, April 27, 1992, pp. 37–39.

35. Gerald Pomper et al., *The Election of 1984* (Chatham, N.J.: Chatham House, 1985), p. 74.

36. Presidential candidate debate, Boston, Mass., October 3, 2000.

37. Cannon, "The Supremes' Future."

38. Jonathan Groner, "The Bush Justices: Pro-Business but Still Independent," *Legal Intelligencer*, October 18, 2000, p. 4.

39. Senator John F. Kerry, "The Case of the Bush Majority vs. Justice and Opportunity," Speech to the National Council of Negro Women, Washington, D.C., October 3, 2003, at http://www.johnkerry.com/pressroom/speeches/spc_2003_1003.html, accessed on January 16, 2004.

40. Stuart Taylor, "Blackmun Has Sharp Opinions of Colleagues," *New York Times*, July 18, 1988, p. A10.

41. See, for example, Henry Reske, "Tracing a Rumor's Spread," *ABA Journal*, August 1992, pp. 34–35; and "Pennsylvania's Senate Race," *Economist*, October 17, 1992, pp. 30–35.

42. The Pew Research Center for the People and the Press, "Public Attentiveness to News Stories: 1986–2002," at http://people-press.org/nii.

Chapter 6

1. For a discussion of this proposal, see Ward, *Deciding to Leave*.

2. Dean, *The Rehnquist Choice*, pp. 37, 59, 81.

3. Abraham, *Justices, Presidents, and Senators*, pp. 9–10, 253; and Terry Eastland, *Energy in the Executive: The Case for the Strong Presidency* (New York: Free Press, 1992), pp. 236–237.

4. Presidential candidate debate, Boston, Mass., October 3, 2000.

5. See David J. Garrow, "Justice Souter Emerges," *New York Times Magazine*, September 25, 1994, p. 52.

6. Paul Simon, *Advice and Consent*, p. 308.

7. *Nomination of Stephen G. Breyer to Be Associate Justice of the Supreme Court of the United States*, p. 384.

8. Ibid.

9. Ibid., pp. 231–232, 240–241.

10. See, for example, his opening statement in the Ginsburg hearings. *Nomination of Ruth Bader Ginsburg to Be Associate Justice of the Supreme Court of the United States*, pp. 30–31.

11. Abraham, *Justices, Presidents, and Senators*, pp. 329–330.

12. One notable exception was the minority counsel on the Senate Watergate hearing, Fred Thompson, who later both pursued a successful acting career and served for eight years as a U.S. senator from Tennessee.

13. See Simon, *Advice and Consent*, p. 306.

14. "An Unacceptable Nominee," *New York Times*, January 29, 2003, p. A26.

15. When Senator Strom Thurmond, then chairman of the Senate Judiciary Committee, asked whether he believed the *Marbury* decision meant that the Congress and the president are subject to the Court's interpretation, Scalia replied: "As I say, *Marbury v. Madison* is one of the pillars of the Constitution. To the extent that you think a nominee would be so foolish, or so extreme as to kick over one of the pillars of the Constitution, I suppose you should not confirm him. But I do not think I should answer questions regarding any specific Supreme Court opinion, even one as fundamental as *Marbury v. Madison*." U.S. Congress, Senate, Committee on the Judiciary, *Hearings for the Nomination of Judge Antonin Scalia to Become Associate Justice of the Supreme Court of the United States*, 99th Congress, 2nd Session, August 5–6, 1986, p. 33.

16. Interview with Justice Stephen Breyer, December 5, 1994.

17. Ibid.

18. Rotunda, "Innovations Disguised as Traditions."

19. *Planned Parenthood of Southeastern Pennsylvania, et al. v. Casey.*

20. Neil A. Lewis, "At the Bar: The Press Is Caught in a Misrepresentation of Clarence Thomas' Words, or Is It?" *New York Times*, December 20, 1991, p. B9.

21. See Patrick M. McFadden, *Electing Justice: The Law and Ethics of Judicial Election Campaigns* (Chicago: American Judicature Society, 1990), pp. 177–188.

22. Ibid.

23. Larry C. Berkson and Seth Anderson, "Judicial Selection in the United States: A Special Report," at http://www.ajs.org/js/materials.htm.

24. Chris Cobb, "Canadians Want to Elect Court," *National Post* (Toronto), February 4, 2002.

25. Michael Delli Carpini and Scott Keeter, *What Americans Know about Politics and Why It Matters* (New Haven, Conn.: Yale University Press, 1996), p. 78.

26. Times Mirror News Interest Index, August 5, 1993.

27. Harris Survey, August 13, 1986.

28. "Bush Engages and Persuades Public on Iraq," Pew Research Center for the People and the Press, September 19, 2002.

29. ABC News/*Washington Post* survey, May 23, 1994; Gallup survey, June 24, 1993; and Harris Survey, August 12, 1968.

30. Roper survey, October 1986 and October 1981.

31. Quinnipiac University Poll, March 5, 2003.

32. *Judicial Selection in the United States: A Compendium of Provision,* 2nd ed. (Chicago: American Judicature Society, 1993), pp. 18–21.

33. John Massaro, *Supremely Political,* p. ix.

34. Ibid., pp. 202–203.

35. "Remarks by the President to Boys' Nation," The White House, Office of the Press Secretary, July 29, 1994.

Index